ADVENTURES WITH CHILDREN

Exploring Ways of Learning & Teaching
in the Church School

MARY CALHOUN

ABINGDON / NASHVILLE

To my Mother, Gussie B. Calhoun,
my first teacher,
who continues to be a growing-learning person
at age eighty-nine.

ADVENTURES WITH CHILDREN

Copyright © 1978 by Abingdon

Library of Congress Cataloging in Publication Data

Calhoun, Mary, 1915-
   Adventures with children.

   Bibliography: p.
   1. Christian education of children. I. Title.
BV1475.2.C318   268'.432   78-715

ISBN 0-687-00925-1

MANUFACTURED BY THE PARTHENON PRESS, AT
NASHVILLE, TENNESSEE, UNITED STATES OF AMERICA

CONTENTS

ACKNOWLEDGMENTS

I am indebted to many persons for my being and becoming as a person, a Christian, a learner and a teacher, a church educator, and writer of this book. Some of these persons are named for specific contributions throughout this book. They and many others have had even greater influence on my life and thoughts leading to the development of this book.

Special words of appreciation are given to
—my housemate and members of my family who have provided love, support, and encouragement through many years;
—persons, in my growing-up years and today, who have surrounded me as a community of faith;
—a friend who served as my on-the-job counselor in planning together for our two second-grade classes;
—executives and co-workers in Christian education, who have both affirmed and challenged my developing ideas on learning and teaching in the church;
—friends, co-workers, and family members who have given theological, educational, and editorial counsel in review of the manuscript for this book.

Mary Calhoun
Director of Children's Education
United Methodist Board of
Discipleship

INTRODUCTION

**You are invited to participate in a venture of
reflection
assessment
anticipation.**

This book offers you some clues for examination of approaches in the church's educational ministry. It is primarily directed to teachers of children in the church school. Parents, pastors, administrators, and other concerned persons also are invited to explore the intent and procedures of the congregation's teaching-learning program for children. Views of learning and of procedures developed in this book are pertinent also to education for youth and adults.

Illustrations of specific learning experiences are identified with young children and older boys and girls. Developmental charts (pages 24-27) apply to persons from birth through sixth grade.[1] Each user of this book—whether concerned with children, youth, or adults—is encouraged to substitute or add illustrations from his or her own experiences or observations.

The clues offered throughout the book for your exploration include
• ways of bringing to mind your own experiences and insights:
• shared thoughts out of the writer's personal experiences, observations, and study:
• identification of some concerns and alternative approaches in Christian education in the past and present;
• projection of possible directions in Christian education for the future.
You are invited to become actively involved in evaluating alternative ways of learning and teaching for the
present and for the future.
Reflect on your own experiences in learning
• to know and respond to God's love:
• to know what it means to be a disciple of Jesus Christ, a Christian;
• to live a Christian life in day-by-day relationships, with the guidance of the Holy Spirit.
Assess ways of learning and teaching in the church:
• your own past and present experiences as learner, as leader;
• approaches you have observed;
• innovative ways of teaching-learning other teachers and groups are exploring and using.
Anticipate the future in Christian education:
• what the future world and child life will be like;
• what that future will offer to or require of persons who seek to live Christian lives;
• how those who teach can help growing boys and girls to live now and in the future in accord with God's love, in response to the life and teachings of Jesus, under the guidance and empowerment of the Holy Spirit;
• how young (and older) learners might find different and better ways of responding to God, and living out their discipleship.

This book is designed to stimulate and give direction to your venture of exploring and reshaping your own views of Christian education for children and older persons. Ideas expressed and questions raised were brought together as I sought to clarify my own present understandings of Christian education and of various approaches in learning and teaching in the church. I offer this written account of my thoughts for whatever help it will be in stimulating or enriching your reflection, study, and development of new insights.

Your venture, whether alone or with other persons, will likely be quite different from mine. Each of us is a unique person with a particular background of experience in growth and learning as a Christian. Each of us has differing perceptions of goals and procedures for learning and teaching in the church. Each of us has her or his own ways of reacting to and processing developing insights.

A personal experience during the time this book was being written will help express my hopes in sharing my quest for understanding and growth with any who might use this book. I was participating in the Children's Forum of the Education for Christian Life and Mission Forums. A man approached me one day. He seemed eager to meet me, for, as he said, "You have been my teacher through your writings on intergenerational learning." Later in the day this same man was serving as resource leader on intergenerational learning opportunities in the church. He announced that he had just met one of his teachers and gave my name. As he continued leading of the group, I could not identify in either his ideas or his procedures any specific teachings of mine. Yet in some way, my writing had been of such value to him that he identified me as his "teacher." [2]

I invite you to
- use this book in dialogue with your own thoughts and experiences,
- explore your own perceptions and convictions,
- reach your own conclusions.

At times you are encouraged to write statements or check ideas in this book. You may wish to use a pencil so that you can revise your responses at a later time. You may prefer to write your responses in a notebook rather than writing in this book.

This venture in guided study is yours! You are in charge of it. Begin where you are most interested.

If you wish to begin with
examining your own teaching style,
go to chapter 7, or chapters 1 and 7. Use the exercises in chapter 7 before going to other sections of the book. Recheck your responses after exploring differing ways of learning and approaches to teaching-learning (chapters 5, 6, 10).

If you want to get a general overview
of ideas and procedures dealt with in this book,
go from the Introduction to chapter 12, "Observations About Learning and Teaching." Review the observations, looking for those with which you agree or disagree, or about which you have questions. Let your responses to those observations provide clues for the chapter or chapters you will use next. After further study return to chapter 12 to affirm or change your earlier responses.

If you are concerned with relating your teaching style and approaches
to an understanding of the child and how he or she learns,
begin with chapter 4, "The Learner and Learning." Then explore ways of teaching in the following chapters.

If you would like to get a perspective
on Christian education,
use Chapter 1 to help you identify your ideas. Then, let chapter 2 spark reflection on your experiences leading to your present understandings of Christian education. Open up some thoughts about the future in Christian education, using chapter 3.

If you would like to compare
some differing ways of directed learning in the church,
explore self-directed, group-directed, and teacher-directed learning, using the charts and descriptions in chapters 5 and 6. Then, review a variety of general approaches for learning and teaching in chapter 9.

**Best wishes
as you continue in creating
your own learning and teaching styles
as a growing Christian
and a leader of learners.**

CHRISTIAN EDUCATION IN THE TWENTIETH CENTURY

SECTION I

1

LEARNING AND TEACHING IN THE CHURCH

Be not the first by whom the new are tried,
Nor yet the last to lay the old aside.
—Pope

Wait!
Innovators are needed,
So are those who ask Why? of change.

As you begin this study, check your present view of what is important in Christian education.

Rank the following statements. Put 1 in front of the statement most nearly expressing your view of what is most important in Christian education. Put 2 and 3 for second- and third-rank statements.

—— Christian education enables the child to grow in knowing what it means to be a Christian (an informed Christian).

—— Christian education enables the child to experience being a Christian empowered by the Holy Spirit (a committed Christian in faith, attitudes, feelings).

—— Christian education enables the child to live a Christian life (a witnessing Christian—relating to God, self, others in accord with one's best understanding of what being a disciple of Jesus Christ means).

Add other ideas if you wish.

Now, look at some *assumptions* about learning end teaching in the church. Do you agree or disagree with the following statements? Are there statements with which you partially agree? What assumptions would you add?

Use the "agree _____ disagree" scale on the right to affirm or challenge the assumptions listed below. Check

1 for agree

6 for disagree or seriously question

2, 3, 4, or **5** for somewhere in between.

If you agree with part, but not all, of a statement, you may want to underline the part with which you **agree** or to revise the part with which you disagree.

Agree ◄————► Disagree
1   2   3   4   5   6

Learning may be one or more of the following:
• acquiring knowledge or information
• gaining insights or understandings
• changing attitudes
• developing or strengthening skills.

— — — — —

The distinctiveness of Christian education is in what knowledge, insights, attitudes, skills are desired and worked toward, and for what purpose. —— —— —— —— —— ——

Interrelationships (learner with leader, learner-learner, learner-situation) are involved in any teaching-learning experience. —— —— —— —— —— ——

Christian education includes both
  • experiential learning in the family, peer group, and congregation; and
  • planned teaching-learning experiences. —— —— —— —— —— ——

Learning experiences in the church may be primarily self-directed, group-directed, or teacher-directed. —— —— —— —— —— ——

Christian educators (curriculum planners, local church administrators, teachers, parents) are all concerned
  • that children grow in the Christian faith, and
  • that children's learning contribute to Christian living. —— —— —— —— —— ——

Christian educators are concerned with both
  • what is to be taught, and
  • how learners are to be involved in learning. —— —— —— —— —— ——

Learners are responsible for their own learning. —— —— —— —— —— ——

Whatever the teaching-learning plans of the teacher(s), the learners make some decisions. Such decisions may be
  • task oriented: what goals to pursue, how work toward those goals, and/or
  • behavioral: initiating own or group activities, following leads of peers, cooperating or not cooperating with leader or group plans. —— —— —— —— —— ——

Each person has her or his own learning style. —— —— —— —— —— ——

The individual's learning style is a product of that person's
  • response to self and to others,
  • independence-dependence tendencies,
  • satisfaction or dissatisfaction with various approaches in learning,
  • ways of organizing thoughts,
  • ease-difficulty in use of learning resources. —— —— —— —— —— ——

Church education is most effective when each learner is enabled in the use of her or his strongest learning skills, and is supported or guided in developing lesser skills. —— —— —— —— —— ——

Goals give direction for planned learning experiences. Leader intention and learner desire may or may not be in accord. These may become the same or be brought into accord through mutually agreed upon goals. —— —— —— —— —— ——

Content provides resource for exploration, development of meaning, interpretation of experience. —— —— —— —— —— ——

Procedures for learning enable or inhibit the learning intended or desired. —— —— —— —— —— ——

Activities provide ways of
  • exploring ideas, suppositions, questions, and
  • expressing one's own ideas, interpretations, feelings, moods. —— —— —— —— —— ——

Learning occurs as the learner uses content, resources, activities for pursuing his or her interests and/or working toward personal or group goals. —— —— —— —— —— ——

Learning takes place also through unplanned experiences—accidents, unexpected encounters, informal relationships, discovery in unanticipated ways. —— —— —— —— —— ——

Each *teacher or teaching team* develops a unique teaching style and a specific teaching-learning plan. —— —— —— —— —— ——

The teacher(s) may use curriculum materials in a variety of ways:
  • following the writer's plan step by step,
  • adapting goals and procedures for the learning group,
  • using these materials as resources for leaders and learners in developing their own goals and learning activities. —— —— —— —— —— ——

Agree ←——→ Disagree
1 2 3 4 5 6

The way(s) in which curriculum materials are used in developing a plan for teaching-learning is related to the teaching style(s) of the teacher(s). — — — — — —

Church leaders can learn from public educators about how children learn and procedures for guiding children in their learning. — — — — — —

Church school teachers, with the help of other church leaders, develop their own plans and procedures. They develop this teaching-learning design in relation to the objective for Christian education (see page 10), and in light of their perceptions of
 • meaning of the gospel for children,
 • specific goals for Christian education,
 • how learners may achieve those goals,
 • how teachers may guide learners in their goal achievement. — — — — — —

Each person who serves as a leader in the church school comes to his or her own understanding of learning and teaching out of
 • his or her own learning and teaching experiences,
 • curriculum materials and other guidance resources available,
 • opportunities for leader development experiences. — — — — — —

Add other assumptions below—your own or ones you have heard other persons express. Check these additional assumptions for agree ←——→ disagree. — — — — — —

— — — — — —

The terms *Christian education, church education,* and *church school* have been used above in identifying assumptions about learning and teaching in the church. Another frequently used term is *Sunday school.* Let's examine what we mean by each of these terms. Each is a useful term when appropriately used.

The ideas below are my understanding of interpretations used by many of the major denominations.

Christian education includes all of a person's learning experiences—in home, church, and elsewhere—which contribute to his or her understanding of the gospel and lead to his or her commitment to Christ and Christian living.

Church education includes all learning experiences within the church and under the guidance of the church. Church education may take place in different kinds of groups: peer, inter-age, congregation, inter-church, inter-faith. It may take place also in the church family and in church-sponsored groups such as scout troops.

Church education includes experiences of learning throughout the life of the congregation in study, in worship, in fellowship, in various boards and committees, in social action, in all phases of ministry and mission.

Church education takes place through the church school with its programs for nurturing, training, enabling growth of persons in Christian faith, in commitment to Jesus Christ, and in fulfilling their discipleship to Christ in daily living.

Church education takes place also through other organizations of the church with specialized goals such as:
 • understanding of global ministry and involvement in mission beyond the local congregation;
 • involvement in social action in and beyond the community, including interpretation, action, reflection;
 • business administration, worship, fellowship.

Church education takes place as persons experience the meaning of being the church—as they deal with conflict, concerns, hopes, dreams in relation to their differing perceptions of the meaning and message of the Christian faith and the gospel of Jesus Christ.

The *church school* is the school of the church providing planned teaching-learning experiences for developing Christians. Its program is designed for

1) enabling the young and the more mature to possess their heritage of the Christian faith and life—drawing from the Bible, the history and tradition of the Christian church, the faith community today in the congregation and in the more inclusive church;

2) enabling each child and older person to know himself or herself as a person of worth, a child of God;

3) equipping each person to live as a responsible human being in relation to self, to others, to the natural world as he or she responds to God's love and to God's will for his or her life.[1]

The *Sunday school* is the school of the church in session on Sunday, usually in the morning preceding or following the congregational worship. Occasionally one hears reference to "our Sunday school meeting on Tuesday afternoon" or at some other weekday time. The Sunday school, then, is the regular once-a-week ongoing study/instruction/discovery/learning sessions of the church school. Sessions on days other than Sunday might more accurately be called the "Tuesday school" or some other identifying name.

The church school includes all formal and informal teaching-learning opportunities under the administration and supervision of the education commission or committee of the church and/or the superintendent of the church school. The church school includes: Sunday (or weekday) school; vacation school; camps; short-term groups for mission study, or other special emphases; interest groups, such as those for music, drama, hobby groups; through-the-week nursery, kindergarten, day care; other settings for learning.

Church education, to be most effective, is intentional—not only in the church school, but also throughout the ministry and mission of the church. The congregation can strengthen its life as a Christian community and its outreach to other persons by developing its structured and informal programs in light of clearly defined goals.

To fulfill its responsibilities in Christian education, the church plans for educational ministry with goals, teaching-learning settings, approaches in learning, designed for achieving the *objective of the church:*

> that all persons be aware of and grow in their understanding of God, especially of his redeeming love as revealed in Jesus Christ, and that they respond in faith and love—to the end that they may know who they are and what their human situation means, increasingly identify themselves as [children] of God and members of the Christian community, live in the spirit of God in every relationship, fulfill their common discipleship in the world, and abide in the Christian hope.[2]

This objective becomes specific as it is made relevant for two-year-olds or four-year-olds, for eights or eighty-eights. At the same time, what is taught must be sound enough to be a foundation for later experience and learning. This objective of the church through Christian education is a continuing objective for lifelong Christian nurture. The church, with this objective, seeks to enable persons, at their own level, to understand and respond to God's self-revelation and to his purposes in all their relationships.[3]

We who are church school leaders are in the business of Christian education, which is in accord with the "gospel according to Jesus," is "God-centered," and "person-oriented." [4] The chapters of this book are designed for helping you, me, and other church leaders search for more effective approaches in Christian education.

Our goal is intentional creation of teaching styles by individual teachers or teaching teams for enabling children (and more mature persons) to achieve the objective of the church for Christian education.

Our context is experiential Christian education—in the family, in the peer group, in the congregation, in the classroom, and elsewhere.

Our focus is, within this broader context of Christian education, on the need for planned teaching-learning experiences.

Our procedure, in this search, is
- to look at who we are as learners and leaders,
- to explore three ways of learning and a variety of approaches for planned learning and teaching in the church,
- to identify factors that will help the teacher(s) plan for present and future teaching-learning experiences with children.

Our concern here is not the old versus the new, but how, from among various teaching-learning approaches, we can select those we and our groups can use most effectively in Christian education.

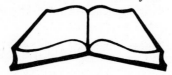

ADVENTURES WITH CHILDREN

2
LOOK BACK TO LOOK AHEAD

Recall of your own experiences in learning and leading will help you focus on
- values you have experienced;
- concerns you have;
- points for affirmation, reinforcement, or change.

What are your observations (reflections) on Christian education thus far in the twentieth century? Particularly in your lifetime?

Thinking of your own experiences in learning and teaching, complete each of the following sentences with three different thoughts.

Learning is _____ .
_____ .
_____ .

Teaching is _____ :
_____ .
_____ .

Christian education is _____ :
_____ .
_____ .

Reflections on Christian education as you have experienced or observed it give you background for your continuing participation and leadership in the church. My experiences and observations are offered
- first, as a stimulus for your reflections, and
- second, as bases for concepts and insights stated in this book.

Christian education in the past sixty years. Each of us has a unique heritage—her or his very personal experiences in living and learning. Your own recalled experiences and observations hold valid meaning for you. I have chosen to focus my reflections on my own lifetime: 1915 to the present.

Ideas expressed throughout this book indicate my thinking at the present time. These thoughts have developed out of my own family and church heritage and my experiences in public education and in the world at large. My understandings of Christian education include perceptions of persons and how learning takes place, theological perceptions, and interpretations of Christian education. These understandings are continually tested, reinforced, or revised through new experiences and additional study and reflection. A sabbatical study centering on alternative approaches in church education stimulated the writing of this book.[1] Responses of reviewers of the first manuscript have sparked additional insights for me and revisions for the book.

Reflection on personal experience and study further affirms or modifies my perception of what learning is and how Christian education takes place.

What are your thoughts on learning, on Christian education? Some of my observations are
- Learning generally comes through a series of experiences.
- A single experience is occasionally powerful enough to result in a new insight or skill.
- Reflection on experience and insights reinforces the learning.
- Many persons contribute to these learning experiences, though only a few of these persons may be identified as teachers.
- Becoming and being a Christian is intertwined with learning physical, mental, and social skills and understandings.

- Persons are whole beings, not segmented parts.
- Relationships of persons to persons are prime factors in each individual's content and style of learning.
- Christian education includes both informal learning and structured or directed learning.
- The Bible and theological understandings are basic in all teaching—learning for Christian commitment and living.

For me, *experiential learning* has come
- through parental guidance with openness to questioning, reasoning, individual and family decision-making, all tempered with clear interpretations of our values as a Christian family. "Our family believes . . ."; "We do . . . because . . ."; "Think about . . . as you make your decision. . . ."
- through support from two older brothers and a younger sister, who not only helped me learn to walk, to swim, to achieve other physical skills, but also enabled me to feel accepted as a person, helped me grow in self-confidence, and provided the give and take of day-by-day learning to live together in Christian love (with counsel and guidance from our parents). "We tease you in love, not in derision."
- through church teachers relating to me, and others in our class, beyond Sunday morning. "Come to my house for a party Saturday afternoon." "We can work on these books Tuesday after school."
- through others in the congregation providing a warm, welcoming, supportive Christian fellowship in week-by-week contacts and in special times of stress or excitement, such as moves from one church to another, my brother's pneumonia, my father's illness and death, my weeks of typhoid fever, my graduation from high school and college. "Come with us to our home." "Congratulations."
- through fellow-teachers in public school and church education who shared concerns, exchanged methods of planning and teaching, and responded to my insights and uncertainties. "We can work on this together."
- through children in their spontaneous expression of ideas and questions, and in their revealing of various feelings of hurt, joy, withdrawal, resistence, hope, openness, freedom to learn. "Why say 'To our Negro friends'? We don't say, 'To our white friends.' Let's just say, 'To our friends'."
- through administrators in volunteer and professional relationships providing reassurances, challenges, resources for exploration and growth, undergirded with Christian love, with acceptance of my personal limitations, and with encouragement for development of my potential. "I take pride in my choice of staff. I know you can do what you have outlined."
- through my peers—as a child, as a public-school and a church-school teacher, as a professional Christian educator—who, through support or conflict, have enabled me to gain new insights, to reconsider and perhaps change or reinforce beliefs, attitudes, values previously held. "Do you really mean that?" "Did you realize why she reacted as she did when you . . . ?"

These persons and many more have been my teachers. Included among those other teachers have been leadership instructors, writers, multi-media developers, friends. With all of these, I have had some degree of control over my learning. How I responded within each situation has been part of my learning experience. What I have done with my own thoughts, feelings, and behaviors out of each situation and the combination of many situations has tempered the learning outcomes.

In reflecting on *planned,* or *directed, learning* in the church, I again draw on personal experience from early childhood to the present.

Your observations of developments in Christian education may be similar to mine, parallel, or quite different. Data you use to validate or test your perceptions may come from some of the same resources I have indicated in footnotes and bibliography. Whether you are a United Methodist or a member of another denomination, you will draw from your own experiences and from additional resources (even as I have) for theories of learning and teaching and for the theological, psychological, educational foundations of Christian education.

On the following pages you will find statements of church education goals, purposes, or objective at different periods of the twentieth century.[2] Most of these statements are from official church documents. They have been basic in the shaping of curriculum for church-school teaching and learning.

After reading each statement for periods in your life time, recall some of your own experiences in those years. Think especially of your church school memories, but include also recollections of other related growing-up experiences. My personal time line may help to stimulate your memories (column 1 of the chart following each goal or objective statement).

Reflect on your thoughts about church school learning and teaching related to your experiences. How are your thoughts similar to or different from mine (column 2 of the chart)?

Aims of Christian education in the early years of the 20th century. Though historically there were no clearly stated goals or objectives, there emerged three identifiable aims:

an evangelistic aim: to win the child to a definite commitment of his or her life to Christ as Savior and Lord and to membership in the church;

an instructional aim: to instruct the child in what he or she needed to know concerning the Christian religion—including Bible study and study of beliefs and denominational practices;

a growth aim: to develop Christian character.[3]

Personal experience time-line of writer	Thoughts on learning and teaching in the church
1915–20 Born into church family, father a minister in Methodist Episcopal Church South (having just changed from law practice), mother, two brothers 1½ and 3 years, 15 months later a sister. Baptized as an infant. Beginner class on front pew with teacher standing in front, following opening period for whole Sunday school. Bible, a familiar book in home and church.	Sunday school—the major setting for church teaching. Teacher as one who knows, children as ones to be taught. Young children learn from the Bible through older persons who find meaning in the biblical content and message.
1921–26 Our second move as a parsonage family. Primary class (combined beginner and primary ages) in one room. Older children, youth, adults in sanctuary, some classes in automobiles when weather permitted. Became full member of the church. Received own Bible from parents on 9th birthday. Father died in 1926; mother employed; grandmother living with us.	Children learn best in age-level groups (broadly graded, group graded, or single graded); content and learning procedures can be more nearly geared to child capabilities. Older children are capable of reading and studying the Bible.
1926–33 Missed 2 months of public school and Sunday school with typhoid fever. Returned to Sunday school in new educational building—six classes in junior department, boys and girls separate. Junior teachers had classes in their homes for additional activities. Junior league with missionary emphasis, children taking part in own programs. Participation in Youth Department activities. Hi Camp and Youth Assemblies. First teaching—intermediate class in vacation school (1932).	Teacher's relationships with class members important—in class and beyond Sunday morning. Time outside of class expands opportunity for relationships and increased learning.

Desires of the church for children in 1930s. Recognizing that Christian character cannot be developed apart from day-by-day living, the church desires for every child:

1) the best possible opportunity for good health, proper food, suitable clothing, and normal bodily development;

2) understanding and treatment as a real person capable of worthy membership in home, community, church, and in the family of God, even while he or she is a child;

3) that he or she shall have the privilege of the best that any of us knows about Christian ways of living;

4) that he or she shall know, love, and trust God, shall feel at home in his or her world, and shall find joy in Christian life and service.[4]

1933–41	
Secretary to forest ranger. College years, preparing for teaching profession. Public school teaching, second grade. Support and counsel from another second-grade teacher.	Emphasis on motivation for learning: teacher provides stimuli, child responds with more interest and greater effort in learning. More variety in teaching methods—storytelling, singing, praying, art activities, others.
Teaching intermediates (junior high) in Sunday school and vacation school. District director of youth work.	Vacation school—more freedom for varied activities, increased consecutive day time, more than one teacher for a class.
Summer term at Scarritt College (1940).	Teaching is more effective when church-school teachers work with natural characteristics and interests of children.
Class in Christian Workers' School on "Evangelism in the Church School" taught by Dr. R. Ira Barnett, Conference Executive Secretary, who later nominated me as Director of Children's Work for the Florida Conference and who guided and nurtured me in that job as a leader of leaders in Christian education.	Child should be nurtured in love of God from birth, knowing himself or herself to be a child of God without being required to name a time when he or she first knew God's love. Evangelism through the church school includes witness, nurture, calling to commitment to Jesus Christ and the Christian church.

The purpose of all Christian education is "that the child may come to know God as ever present and all-loving and Christ as Lord and Savior, and increasingly identify himself with Christian purposes and enterprises." [5]

These purposes of Christian nurture were identified under the following areas:

• relationship with God and ideas of God,
• relationship with Jesus and ideas of Jesus,
• the child and the church fellowship,
• the child's heritage in the Bible,
• the child in his personal relationships,
• the child in his social relationships,

Purposes of Christian nurture (in some lists) included also

• growth in Christ-like character.

1941–54	
Conference director of Children's Work in Florida Conference, The Methodist Church—Conference included churches of all three former branches: Methodist Episcopal, Methodist Episcopal Church South, Methodist Protestant.	Goals and methods of teaching interrelated—teaching love through love, faith in God through sharing one's faith . . .
Program planning for workers with children in churches of the conference. Teacher training schools as instructor.	Christian education makes use of understandings of the nature and development of the child in guiding children in Christian knowledge and growth.
	Varied teacher reactions to church-school units on God, Jesus, Bible, and those on church and on

Administration and leadership in vacation school institutes, laboratory schools, and other teacher training schools.

Attendance at jurisdictional leadership enterprises and national programs such as Methodist Conference on Christian education. Some leadership responsibilities in these.

Winter term at Garrett Biblical Institute (1949).

One year leave from conference to complete work toward masters degree in religious education (1952) at Boston University.

Leadership in training events in other Conferences, as well as in Florida.

personal and social relationships. Those reactions raised questions about what Christian education is.
• Is it limited to knowledge about or relationship to God, Jesus, Bible?
• What does it have to do with church history, with being the church today?
• How does it relate to personal and social life and relationships?

The Bible is not only a special book about God and about men's responses to God; it is a book about God's action in creation, in individuals, and in the life of the tribe or nation. It is a guide to Christian life and character. Teaching the Bible involves both studying the content of the Bible and relating the Bible message to experience.
Biblical teaching includes use of Bible in helping children gain
• clearer ideas of God and Jesus,
• understandings of God's action in the world,
• understandings of Christian views of life and God's will for persons,
• guidance for Christian living.

The church has a responsibility through parent education for nurture of children in family.
The church, through Christian education, enables children to have a sense of belonging in the community of believers in Christ—a community that offers love, support, call to Christian discipleship in all areas of life.

Teacher uses stories, pictures, Bible passages, objects, relationships within the class in helping children gain new insights and meaning.
Children learn through atmosphere of room; child-size equipment enhances child comfort, interest, and learning potential.

A child-oriented room—appropriate equipment, cheerful room, pictures and other resources—says to the child, "You are inportant in this church. We care about you."
Children need opportunities to know minister as "our pastor."
Two or more teachers (leader and assistant or co-teachers) expand teacher-child relationships and can exemplify Christian living in teacher-to-teacher relationships.

Teaching is more than imparting knowledge or transmitting the faith by telling—it is leading, guiding, developing, enabling children in discovering, thinking, reaching conclusions in their own search for faith and meaning.

Children learn through a variety of experiences with literature, especially the Bible and church history. They learn also through music, art, creative activities; through relationships with other persons; and through accepting and carrying out responsibilities.

Worship is most meaningful when integrated with other learning experiences. Church education includes both spontaneous and planned worship. Christian education is concerned also with stewardship of body, time, talents, possessions, natural world.

The *purposes of the Christian religion* as accomplished *through* the processes of *education* . . . :

1. To make God a reality in human experience; to give individuals a sense of personal relationship to him.
2. To develop an understanding and appreciation of the personality, life and teachings of Jesus.
3. To foster Christlike character through progressive and continuous development.
4. To make the fatherhood of God and the brotherhood of man the motivation underlying the social order.
5. To develop in growing persons the disposition and the ability to participate in the organized society of Christians—the Church.
6. To develop in growing persons an appreciation of the meaning and importance of the Christian family, and the ability and disposition to participate in and contribute constructively to the life of this primary social group.
7. To lead all into recognizing God's purpose and plan in life and in the universe, and into appreciating each person's essential part in God's plan.
8. To help man assimilate the best religious experience of the race, preeminently that recorded in the Bible, as the guide to present experience.[6]

1954–64

Member of national staff in Christian education of children, Board of Education, The Methodist Church.

Relationships with program and editorial staffs of The Methodist Church and of other denominations in program planning and curriculum development.

Participation in The Methodist Conference on Christian Education and other national educational events.

Work with conference and district leaders in children's work.

Leadership in laboratory schools, coaching conferences, laboratory seminars, and other training events for beyond-the-local-church leaders.

Educational consultant for production of *Breakthru,* TV series for older children.

Through Christian education the church seeks to help boys and girls grow in relationships with God and with other persons and also in self-understanding and self-worth.

Adults (teachers) and children are members together in "our class"—each person both learner and teacher.

Children and teachers have varying group member roles and responsibilities. Teachers have additional responsibilities in guiding individuals and group in learning-teaching experiences.

The church is concerned that children have a faith of their own—nurtured but not dictated—a faith that includes beliefs and principles by which one lives—a faith for living rooted in a faith in God.

TV offers learning setting different from the classroom. It elicits more involvement of child than does the radio. Educational TV can use some—not all—classroom teaching techniques. It necessitates some procedures distinctive for this media.

The *objective for Christian education* is that all persons be aware of God through his self-disclosure, especially his redeeming love as revealed in Jesus Christ, and that they respond in faith and love—to the end that they may know who they are and what their human situation means, grow as sons of God rooted in the Christian community, live in the spirit of God in every relationship, fulfill their common discipleship in the world, and abide in the Christian hope.[7]

In moving toward this objective the church seeks to help persons deal with basic fundamental questions: Who am I? Why am I here? Where am I going? Who is God? Who is my neighbor? Areas of curriculum (vantage points for experiencing the three dimensions of reality—divine, human, natural—in light of the gospel) are
 • life and its setting: meaning and experience of existence,
 • revelation: meaning and experience of God's self-disclosure,
 • sonship: meaning and experience of redemption,
 • vocation: meaning and experience of discipleship,
 • the church: meaning and experience of Christian community.

1965–77

Continued on national staff in children's ministry, with responsibility for education in
 • Board of Education, The Methodist Church,
 • Board of Education, The United Methodist Church, following merger of The Evangelical United Brethren Church and The Methodist Church, 1968.
 • Board of Discipleship, The United Methodist Church, following restructure of national boards, 1972.

Counseling teacher in local church (several years in grades 3 and 4, then in grades 1 and 2).
Consultant with church groups experimenting with innovative approaches in teaching. Co-leader in experimental laboratory schools using varied approaches.

Continuing involvement in denominational and interdenominational curriculum planning.

Brief sabbaticals with study focus on: impact and potential of TV for Christian education, value development and affective learning, alternative educational approaches.

Christian education takes place at crossing points of the gospel message and life experiences, in interrelating of biblical meaning and living.
In Christian education, we are concerned with
 • purposes, desired outcomes related to objectives
 • beliefs, convictions, doctrine
 • attitudes, behavior
 • relationships

Ministry with children includes —not only educational ministry but also the involvement of children in ministry to and with others.

The child (and older person) experiences, responds, grows, as a whole being; she or he is not segmented in parts. Physical, mental, social, and spiritual development are interrelated.
Persons of different generations learn with and from one another—intergenerational groups expand learning opportunities not only for children but also for youth and adults.

Children live in, and are influenced or molded by, a multi-dynamic world of everyday living and TV impact. Learning, valuing, responding, or reacting are implicit in childrens experiencing of their own expanding world.
Christian education and the church in its total ministry confront children with the gospel message for them and help them discover and respond to leadings of the Holy Spirit as they interact with their total world of daily life.

What were some of your earliest thoughts about what Christian education is all about? What ideas have been reinforced through the years? What understandings have you changed or modified?

How do you see Christian education in the years ahead? In chapter 3 we project our thoughts into the future. What will the world be like? What will Christian education be for the child in that world?

3

CHRISTIAN EDUCATION IN THE COMING YEARS

What are your anticipations, concerns, dreams,
hopes for church education in the remainder of this
century? In the next ten to fifteen years?

Christian education in the future will be what you, I, and other learners and leaders cause it to be. We can just let it happen, or we can be intentional about what Christian education should be and how we can influence church education in that direction.

You might want to anticipate the world and church in the remainder of this century up to the year 2000. Or you may want a shorter projection—perhaps, to the year 1980, the bicentennial year of the church school.

My look ahead is focused on the next ten to fifteen years. This time is selected because of recent and present involvement with other church educators in projecting what Christian education is, should be, and can be in the remainder of the 1970s and through the 1980s.

For use in thinking about children and church education in the years ahead, divide a sheet as indicated below. Column 1 is for your expectations of what the world will be like for children and their families. Columns 2 and 3 are for your concerns and for your dreams and hopes for the church and for Christian education with children.

World of 1978 to——	The church in those years	
Expectations	Concerns	Dreams/Hopes

Our *expectations* for life in the years ahead are rooted in individual and group experiences from the past (see chapter 2) and our observations of trends in the present.[1]

In a recent Children's Forum[2] we were asked to list ideas on "What do you think the world will be like in 1985?" Responses to that question were grouped in several areas having implications for Christian education. These expectations for the next decade are summarized below.

Family structure, population structure . . . less permanent, freer; hesitancy to bring children into family . . . more communal living, smaller families, continued valuing of parent role . . . ambivalence as to fewer or more children . . . zero population growth among affluent families . . . more apartment living . . . legal pressure to control size of family in lower-economic-status families . . . changes in family life-styles not as radical as predicted in sixties . . . more tolerance of variety, more search for stability, new form of extended family (involving neighbors rather than relatives) . . . choices of family life-style and family structure based on who we are rather than on tradition.

Economic situation . . . simpler life-style, more sharing, continuing movement toward elimination of hunger; world economic system which is forced rather than resulting from religious concern . . . inflation, more credit-card buying, more selfishness in buying . . . more capitalism or socialism or a new system.

Work and Leisure . . . more acceptance of validity and worth of leisure activities . . . advance of personal creativity . . . in labor, division of labor, sharing of menial jobs, more human-oriented work (as compared with production-oriented) . . . shorter work week.

Education . . . trend toward individualized education . . . private schools . . . experiential learning . . . more continuing education . . . education for living together, for changing careers, for personhood . . . fewer funds for education, throwing persons back on own resources . . . more creative, ethical training through schools . . . more varied forms of schooling.

Values, value system . . . radical change in value system, high regard for human industry, valuing of heritage and arts . . . more influence in values, morals from industry by default of schools and churches . . . property-oriented values . . . many kinds of values available . . . differences more emphasized . . . more confrontation, crisis; persons may be forced to make more commitment to own values . . . creative acceptance of pluralism or danger of chaos . . . conformity within social strata.

Which ideas above strike you as realistic readings of present trends and possible future trends? What other ideas did you include in your list of expectations of the future?

With your own list of expectations before you, now look at your *concerns* in Christian education. Compare your concerns with those listed below from the Children's Forum.

Concern . . . more shopping for a congregation, looking for homogeneity or support . . . lessening of denominational lines . . . increased leisure, Monday holidays, second home, multiplicity of jobs affecting attendance of church programs . . . possibility of more attention to "being the church" rather than "going to church" with (a) focus on living as the church more than on attendance at eleven o'clock service and (b) more celebration of rites and rituals at times other than Sunday morning at eleven o'clock.

Concern . . . not how to get people back to church so the church can survive, but how can the church identify the needs of persons and society to which the congregation (or denomination or larger church) can minister . . . how the church can meet those needs.

Problem . . . the church, as well as individuals and society, is in an identity crisis . . . are we willing to accept that form follows function, to design church structure and program in terms of who we are as Christians living in this decade . . . what are our intentions about the future of children and older persons, of the church, of society, of the world.

Problem . . . age-level isolation: smaller families, less relationship between teen-agers and children; youth moving toward parenthood without familiarity with children . . . separation of children and old people . . . decrease in extended families with many relatives nearby . . . how might church be catalyst for inter-age, intergenerational relationships for persons of all ages.

Concern . . . how church can support / strengthen each child in his or her own sense of self-worth as a child of God, in dignity as a human being, in feeling of being able to control his or her present and influence the future (e.g., sensitizing adults to children that the dignity of children be enhanced; child-adult relational model as fellow members vs. authoritarian adult-molding-the-child model) . . . different age groups doing things together . . . church as the child's extended family.

No longer is delineation of rights and wrongs or of acceptable and unacceptable behavior an adequate guide for living—if it ever was! Persons through the centuries have been influenced not only by church education but also by family life and family values; by peer experiences and ways of thinking and behaving; by community culture, mores, expectations. In recent years television and other media have brought into the range of influences varied life-styles, world issues, national and international views and value systems.[3]

With your own assumptions, expectations, and concerns in mind, move now with me to some *dreams and hopes* for Christian education in the years ahead.

As I think of the children (and older persons) whom the church seeks to guide through Christian education, I see *each person as responsible for his or her own life direction, own values, own relationships,* finding guidance, support, undergirding from the Christian community for

- intentional decision-making about one's life-style as a child of God;
- discovering who one is, where one is, where one wants to go as a Christian responsible for his or her own actions;
- developing one's own values and value system in light of the gospel of Jesus Christ.

Values that determine how a person responds in various life situations result from hammering out one's own style of life in one's own set of surroundings with influences from other persons who are also developing their unique life-styles.

One hope for the future, then, is that the Christian community may be a primary subculture or learning setting for the child. A related hope is that the church will offer to the child the total Christian community and congregational life as his or her experiencing-learning arena—including the church school as one part of that arena, but not limiting church education to the school model.

A dream for the 1970s and 1980s is for church education that helps each person achieve a life-style that is Christian. By Christian life-style, I mean the way this person lives his or her own life:
- knowing and responding to God's love, as revealed in Jesus Christ,
- responding to the Holy Spirit as enabler of persons,
- making intentional decisions, as a child of God, in commitment to Christ, in his or her own self-actualization and in relationships with other persons.

The church today and the people it seeks to educate are faced with a pluralistic society, rapid change, and an unpredictable future. We cannot assume that to know one's heritage is to know how to live as a Christian. Nor can we assume that one can live as a Christian without knowing his or her heritage. Moreover, we cannot assume that the rules for living used in preceding generations are sufficient for the unpredictable experiences to be confronted in this new age.

Another hope for the future, therefore, is that the church will help each person achieve a Christian life—not by transmitting a set of values to be accepted or rejected, but by providing resources and a supporting fellowship for children and more mature persons as they determine their own values, affirm those values, and act in accord with those values.

Purpose and goals of Christian education for the years ahead: Christian education is concerned with the whole of a person's being and living in all relationships—with self, with God, with other persons, with the natural world.

The *purpose* of Christian education in the 1970s and 1980s is to enable each person
- to experience the reality and love of God,
- to respond to him in faith and love, and
- to make an intelligent commitment to him

so that

the individual will become fully human, experiencing his or her own highest potential
- through self-identity and self-affirmation as a person of worth, a unique child of God;
- through recognition and affirmation of Jesus Christ as the supreme revelation of God;
- through development of a life-style based on values chosen and affirmed in light of the person's own best understanding of what being a disciple of Jesus Christ requires of him or her;
- through involvement in the development and continuation of a Christian community that ministers to persons within and beyond its membership; and
- through participation / action in solving issues and problems of the community (both church and world) in ways consistent with one's own faith response to God and one's own life-style.

If this be the church's purpose, then its *goals for nurture of persons* will be that the church—through the family, through the church school, through the life of the congregation—will:
1. enable each individual to make a conscious, intelligent faith response to God and to develop his or her own life commitment to Jesus Christ and the church;
2. enable each individual, through experiences in and support from the Christian community, to learn to be a person (full humanization) and to develop his or her own approach to daily living (life-style) in which he or she may live out a personal faith in an unpredictable world;
3. help each person see all of his or her life experiences and relationships as input for understanding of self and of personal goals in life;
4. help each person assess, in light of the gospel, values held by various groups in which he or she participates as part of the process of determining his or her own values;
5. involve persons in the life and outreach of the Christian community as a means of fulfilling their own responsibility as committed Christians;
6. enable persons to attain a global perspective; educate persons to be world citizens; involve persons in concern for the needs of others and the necessity of liberation for some; free persons that they might transform society and our social, economic, and political systems;

7. help each person to validate the discovery of his or her own identity in relation to mankind—who I am in terms of (a) history, (b) biblical heritage, (c) culture, (d) social systems, (e) changing experiences, (f) perspective of the world.

Further, the church's *program goals* will be to:
1. provide activities designed to let the person see himself or herself and get feedback on what and who he or she is:
   • in the total Christian community,
   • in family clusters where the individual's habits and traditions are supported and reaffirmed or revised,
   • in intergenerational groups with divergent value systems,
   • in action groups where accumulated reinforced learnings are modified or discarded,
   • in ongoing study groups with persons of one's own age where both emotion and hard work are involved;
2. recognize and intentionally make use of the peak experiences of each person—his or her wonder, awe, fascination, absorption, rapture, enthusiasm, fear, apprehension, discouragement—as the moments in the learning process during which cognitive and personal growth take place simultaneously;
3. acknowledge acts of celebration of God's presence among us and worship of God as learning experiences that in turn may give rise to another cycle of peak experiences;
4. provide for learning experiences centered in the life of the total congregation and moving out into the life of the community.

In working toward these goals, the church *program plans* will include opportunities for
1. persons to theologize, to consciously and intelligently think through and appropriate meanings into understanding and experience;
2. individuals and groups to use the Bible, exploring its message as a basic resource for insight and action as Christians;
3. self-directed or individualized exploration of areas of personal and group concern—with a wide variety of resources for use in exploration, in expression of ideas and feelings, in decision-making action;
4. action-service-witness activities, in which the person's discovery of how he or she is different from others becomes intertwined with the discovery of how he or she is similar to others;
5. participation of individuals in the life of the congregation as it explores alternatives for the future, makes decisions, and takes action for change in accord with the member's best understanding of God's will and purpose.

Implementation of these goals and program plans will require
1. leaders, teachers, helpers, or counselors who can accept the person and help him or her learn what potentialities God has already given—who permit the person to express his or her own thoughts and feelings, to experiment, to act, and even to make mistakes;
2. leaders who function as facilitators of learning,
   • enabling the learner(s) to work independently and interdependently, with initiative and creativity;
   • making available appropriate resources;
   • participating with individuals or learning groups as fellow learners;
   • being open and honest in their own faith and their continuing search for meaning and depth of experience;
3. resources that are varied, current, designed for use in more than one setting; resources that utilize many media; an adequate library of well prepared, carefully selected resources and related equipment; and materials for creative development of resources by individuals and groups;
4. incorporation of major concerns of the church and utilization of the resources and energies of all boards and agencies of the church;
5. leadership development opportunities, training enterprises, and leader guidance resources that are congruent with a learning-to-be-a-person approach in Christian education, offering opportunities for creative, personalized leader-learner experiences; including nurture of the leader's own faith;
6. more mature members of the congregation (adults, youth) who are aware of their role and who accept their responsibility in communicating the faith through informal relationships with young boys and girls and through participation with children in varied learning experiences.

A Christian's life is personal. It is unique for each person as that person lives his or her own life in whatever situations he or she faces. The teaching ministry of the church *(didache)* offers to the individual the power of the proclamation of the gospel *(kerygma)*, strength of the Christian community *(koinonia)*, and opportunities for service (diakonia). Each persons responds with his or her own degree of commitment expressed in and through his or her own life as a Christian, as he or she experiences the continuing, illuminating presence of God through the Holy Spirit.

The future of the church and of Christian education is in our hands, in our minds, in our hearts—yours, mine, and those of other persons in the local congregation, in the denomination, in the interdenominational community, in the world church. Christian education in the years ahead will be shaped by our concerns and by our hopes and dreams to the extent that we express our commitment to Christ through the educational ministry of his church.

In chapter 2 we reflected on Christian education in our life-time to date (for me, the past sixty years; for you, a longer or shorter time). In this chapter we have anticipated the future of Christian education in the years ahead—the next decade, the remainder of the twentieth century. We have seen Christian education as taking place in many ways, in many settings. We have expressed hope that each person's experiences contribute to that person's understanding of the gospel for his or her own life and to the individual's commitment to Christ and to Christian living.

In the remaining chapters of this book, we direct our exploration more specifically to Christian education through planned teaching-learning experiences of the church school.

TEACHING AND LEARNING IN THE CHURCH
SECTION II **SCHOOL**

THE LEARNER AND LEARNING

In this chapter we give our attention to the child (or older person)—*who this person is and how he or she learns, grows, develops as learner in church education.*

A study of the person throughout life, or even of the child, warrants broader coverage than any one book can provide. Several books on life-span development are included in the bibliography. Here my intention is for us to bring to mind what you and I already know or believe about children and how they learn. Perhaps, in this interplay of your thoughts and my writings you will develop some new insights or meaning in your understandings of children and their growth needs.

Much of the material throughout this book is pertinent to youth and adults, as well as to children. This is especially true of chapters 1 and 2, where we consider concepts about Christian education. For this study, however, we focus on the child rather than attempt a lifelong look at the person and his or her development through Christian education.

Use the following ideas or some other means of reflecting on very specific child learning experiences (in the home, church, or elsewhere).

1. Note one of your own early or later childhood experiences where you felt learning took place. Describe that experience:

- where you were_____
- what the situation was_____
- who was there with you_____
- what happened_____
- how this experience related to previous experiences or other situations_____

2. Recall a situation when a child expressed an idea that to you indicated she or he had gained a new insight, or a situation in which the child's behavior showed evidence of change in attitudes or relationships:
   - who the child was _____; age_____; other pertinent information____
   _____
   - what the situation was_____
   - what the child said or did_____
   _____
   - your perception of what led the child to this new understanding or new way of behaving_____
   _____

I think of a second-grade boy in an early elementary class in vacation school. The unit was on growth as part of God's plan. This child was responsive in various activities—planting seeds to watch them grow, making a puppet—but never participating verbally. If we had been depending entirely on verbal communication, this child would have been limited to listening.

He became involved in a puppet play with two girls. His puppet was in the hospital. Their puppets planted seeds to grow flowers for his puppet. They came to the hospital and said, "We brought you some flowers." His puppet moved slightly, but no sound was heard until one of the girls popped up from behind the table and reported, "He said thank you."

Each day on arrival he and other children went immediately to their cups of seeds to see if any had sprouted. One morning, to his great delight, this boy found tiny sprouts in his cup. Some of the teachers and children gathered around to see his plants. A teacher began to sing a familiar song; others joined in. This boy's voice was clearly heard singing, "Deep in the ground a little seed lay wondering what it would be some day. . . ."

From your two illustrations and this one of mine, list factors affecting child learning. Think of other children and other learning situations. You might include some general information such as age, number of children in family or class. Include also very specific ideas, such as child of another nationality in home or class. I've started a list below. What would you add?

Factors affecting child learning:
- active involvement in learning situation
- satisfaction in what the child did
- increasing ease in the group
- sense of achievement
- support and encouragement from other persons
-

Denominational staff members, as well as local church leaders, are concerned about finding more effective ways of involving young children, older boys and girls, youth, and adults in experiencing the Christian gospel and responding to God's love. We are continually seeking better understandings of persons and how they learn. From time to time, national staff (denominationally or interdenominationally) set aside time for concentrated study. The chart on the following pages, "The Children We Teach," comes from one of these staff studies.

In the late sixties and early seventies, the Section of Life Span and Family Education entered into a study of lifelong growth and development of the whole person with particular attention to religious development.[1] In that study, we drew from

- our own cumulative experiences with persons at a given age, and persons from age to age throughout life;
- our individual and collective previous study and testing of various views of personhood and development and of learning theories;
- current personal and group study of theological, psychological, sociological, and educational views of persons and their growth;
- dialogue with resource persons from the fields of theology, psychology and sociology.

THE CHILDREN WE TEACH

The statements on this chart are generalization. Each child is different, a unique person. His/her development is a continuing, ongoing process, with spurts and slow growth periods. Each child's development is influenced by his/her heritage, physical health, and the kind of relationships he/she has with other people, especially the adults in his/her life.

	The Age Definition Physical Development	Interest in Knowledge	Knowledge and Use of the Bible
Birth through 2 years	Infants, Toddlers. Members of the Nursery Home Roll and Nursery 2s. Learns to grasp, to sit up, to stand, to crawl, to walk in the first ten to fourteen months. Learns a few words. Triples birth weight in first two years. Eyes learn to focus. Developing large muscle coordination. Has difficulty with eye-hand coordination.	Explores space and objects in space. Uses all five senses. Learning to use words and short phrases to communicate. Beginning to cope with the complexities of life. Needs help in sorting out acceptable behavior.	Sees parents, teachers use the Bible. Experiences biblical teachings through relationships with persons who live the Bible message. Hears brief Bible stories, verses, and songs. Begins to realize the Bible is a special book that tells about God and Jesus.
3, 4, and 5 years	Nursery 3s and 4s and Kindergarten at church school. Many five-year-olds are in public school and private kindergartens. Some three- and four-year-olds are in day care centers and nursery schools under private auspices. Is mastering finer motor skills, skipping, hopping and throwing a ball, running, climbing. Is mastering conversational skills.	Can speak in sentences. Ask many questions to gain information. Has great imagination. Intuition, rather than logic, is used in thinking process. Gives evidence of desire to learn; e.g. counting, reading.	Learns that the Bible is an important book. Hears Bible stories about persons who tried to live as God wanted them to live. Realizes the most important stories in the Bible are about Jesus. Handles the Bible, sometimes pretending to read a verse. Says or sings Bible verses. "Read to me" books may include Bible stories, verses, related pictures and songs. Observes older persons using Bible in home and church. Experiences Biblical climate of belonging, forgiveness, law, creation and worship.
6, 7, and 8 years	Younger and middle elementary groups in church school. Entering first grade in school or has had a year or more beyond kindergarten. An "in-between" age. Restless, active, energetic, yet tires easily. Eager to learn, but limited by his/her learning skills. In a period of slow physical growth. Bodily growth somewhat stabilized, has acquired the basic proportions of an older child.	Is in a period of concrete thinking. Still functioning primarily in spontaneous, intuitive thought. Sometimes expresses insights which appear to be logical generalizations, but does this spontaneously. Expresses (symbolizes) ideas or feelings in various art forms or in words, but usually is not able to interpret meaning of the symbols. From about 7 years is able to group or classify some things when this can be done on basis of concrete experiences. At about 8 or 9 years begins to move	Begins to understand that the Bible is about people long ago. Learning two parts of Bible: Old and New Testaments. Begins to understand some Bible passages. Anticipates being able to understand more as he/she grows older. Growing interest in having "my own Bible." Beginning to learn how to find a few Bible passages. Uses selected verse or passage as litany response or as choral reading.

Adapted from the chart "Children Learn—Because We Care," in *Planbook for Leaders of Children, 1978-79.* [2]

Awareness of Self Sense of Life Work	Relationships with Others	Relationships with God Sense of the Meaning of Life
Developing a sense of trust or mistrust of others. Learning self-control. Learning to respond in terms of the expectations of adults. Interested in all of his/her body. Learning to cope with toileting. Self-centered—everything is "me" or "mine." Shows temper at times, but is quick to forget. Trying to be independent, but is still dependent on adults. Imitates adults, usually the mother figure. Interprets adult behavior in play. Plays the role of familiar workers in the community. Does not understand work of the parent unless he/she sees it performed.	Experiences the larger world through the mother or mothering figure. Imitates adults. Shy of strangers. Exerts power of self—"me, mine." Learning skills of the culture, feeding self, toileting, dressing, undressing. Responds to expected social behavior. Communicates through behavior. Beginning to understand the rights of others, and to relate to others as friends.	Beginning a life-long growing relationship with God. Begins to experience prayer as he/she hears parents, teachers talk naturally and spontaneously with God. Experiences God's love through loving, caring persons who know God's love in their own lives. Begins to associate name Jesus with certain pictures and with the Bible. Knows Jesus primarily as one who taught about God, helped people, and loved children. Is learning to accept values of adults with whom he/she lives. Is developing a sense of trust or mistrust depending upon trustworthiness of adults. Experiences forgiveness through loving and caring adults.
Continues to test his/her will against others. Seeks acceptance of peers and adults. Experiences guilt as he/she tries to meet adult expectations. Often feels rejected with the arrival of a new brother or sister, or in the presence of another child receiving adult attention. Shows evidence of ability to plan and carry out simple activities. Becomes self-assured in ability to do things. Plays out role of workers with purpose and with longer time span than before.	Sensitive to feelings and rights of others. Engages in quarreling, but for short duration. Enjoys group activities for short periods of time. Plays well with peers, but sometimes becomes assertive. Is distinguishing role of father and mother. Depends on and enjoys family activities. Can take responsibility for simple household duties. Relates to the mother figure, sharing joys and hurts. Eating and sleeping habits fairly well formed. Practices of personal cleanliness being established.	Begins to experience a belonging as a child of God. Begins to be aware of ways persons know God loves them. Asks simple questions about the nature of God, death, birth, crises. Cannot put thoughts of God, church, and other abstract concepts into words, but seems to store up impressions of them. Accepts values and limits of parents and teachers. Able to think about his/her behavior and to improve it. Copes with attitudes of forgiveness and reconciliation. Works on skills of relating to others in terms of practices interpreted by adults as Christian. Relates some experiences of awe, wonder to God as creator of the natural world.
Is learning to cope with self in new situations with varying reactions from teachers and peers. Is no longer a baby entirely dependent on adults, but is far from mature emotional independence. Sees self as attractive or unattractive (physically), as capable or inadequate. Self image is based primarily on perceptions of reactions of family members to him/her. Is generally outgoing and loving unless earlier experiences of rejection cause him/her to be withdrawn or rebellious. Excited about going to school, but sometimes	Is affectionate to those he/she loves: parents, teachers, children. Seeks acceptance, understanding, encouragement, love. Basic dependence and loyalty are shifting from parents to teachers. Facing some degree of conflict in values and expectations of other persons. Conforms (generally) to cultural expectations of a boy or a girl. Acts out in play mores of the culture. Mirrors values of adults. Enjoys playmates from both sexes. Chooses best friend from own sex, but	Accepts uncritically almost everything he/she is told about God. Beginning to ask some "how" and "why" questions. Responsive to God at feeling level or in terms of what he/she has been told, without being able to think logically about God or to express feelings verbally. Asks simple questions about God, wanting simple answers. Not yet able to think through concepts of God. Experiences awe, wonder, appreciation in relation to life cycle of persons, other creatures, growing plants. Relates these to God as creator.

	The Age Definition Physical Development	Interest in Knowledge	Knowledge and Use of the Bible
6, 7, and 8 years continued	Completing change from baby to permanent teeth. Highly susceptible to childhood diseases. Usually has moved beyond exploration of his/her own body as a physical being, but not yet conscious of self as a sexual being. Conscious of "I can" "I can't" accomplishments.	toward the logical thought processes of later years (abstractions and generalizations). Is confused by too early verbalization of religious concepts before he/she can handle insights needed for understanding these concepts.	Learns some verses through use in conversation, story, worship. May receive Bible from church at beginning of third or fourth grade. Recognizes that Bible verses and stories can help him/her remember to be loving, kind, etc.
9, 10, and 11 years	Middle and older elementary groups in church school. Generally fourth, fifth and sixth grades in public school. Wide differences in physical development may raise questions in minds of individual boys and girls about their physical adequacy. May be maturing sexually and having questions about his/her body and/or emotional urges related to sexual development. Girls are likely to mature earlier than boys.	Begins to challenge what adults say is truth. No longer gullible enough to accept whatever is told him/her. A realist. Can be reasoned with. Reading and some other academic skills perfected during this age period. Interested in trying to do things well. Tends to be a perfectionist. Able to use reading in seeking and sharing information. Attention span greatly increased. May spend several hours at an activity if really interested.	Uses Bible in study and worship. Growing awareness and understanding of relation of Bible message to his/her own attitudes and actions. Explores meaning of some biblical passages, through study and discussion. Learning how to use Bible references and the table of contents to locate passages. Becoming acquainted with different sections of Bible (law, Gospels) and where to find these. Learning how the Bible came to be, kinds of literature it contains. Interested in using different translations and versions of the Bible. Begins using reference books such as Concordance and Bible Dictionary. Uses a variety of activities to gain understanding of Bible, Bible history, and biblical message.

Perhaps, at this point, you will want to add some ideas of your own to the chart on the previous pages if you did not do this while reviewing the chart.

Now think again of the present-day child you described at the beginning of this chapter—her or his characteristics as a growing person. Note points at which that child
• shows abilities, characteristics attributed in the chart to her or his age or grade level: _____
• is continuing learning experiences shown in the chart as characteristic of an earlier age:_____
_____
• is more like the description of an older child:_____
_____

Does the child you have in mind have any special needs for additional help or extra opportunities in learning? Is she or he a slow learner? Or an accelerated learner? Is she or he mentally retarded? Does the child have any physical handicaps: limited vision or blindness, hearing deficiency, a crippling condition? Does she or he have special emotional difficulties?

Think of at least two other children in the same group, or community, as the child above. In what ways are the characteristics and learning capabilities of these two children
• similar to those of the first child?_____
_____
• different from that child's?_____
_____

Awareness of Self Sense of Life Work	Relationships with Others	Relationships with God Sense of the Meaning of Life
disappointed at slowness of learning in school. Interested in investigating, experimenting, exploring. Anxious to try new activites, but often frustrated by attempting things beyond his/her capabilities. Growing in ability to make choice decisions. Can sometimes choose between two wishes, one immediate and one delayed.	shifts easily and frequently from one best friend to another. Feels hurts deeply, but forgets quarrels or hurts quickly. Is concerned for hurts of others. Wants to participate in games. Often adamant about rules but easily upset when game does not go his/her way. Aware of similarities and differences in persons. Acceptance/rejection of others easily influenced by adults, peers.	Expresses brief prayers spontaneously if has been helped earlier to verbalize own ideas and feelings in prayer. Looks beyond parents to teachers for authority. Is usually definite in his/her likes-dislikes, wants—don't wants. Unbothered by contradictory ideas or actions, dealing only with the immediate situation.
Becoming increasingly independent of adults. Tends to accept values of peer group rather than adults. Wants to make own decisions. Has developed distinct personality. Is "putting self together," integrating self. Is fairly responsible and dependable. Wants hard work to do, wants to be useful. Wants to serve others. Wants to do something about the wrongs in his/her community. Often speaks of what he/she would like to be when grown up. Growing ability to evaluate way in which others have invested their lives.	Is experimenting with acceptable ways of relating to other persons—with peers of both sexes, youth, adults (parents, teachers, etc.). Feels intensely about unfairness, injustice and social evils. Has a strong sense of right and wrong. Interested in and informed about people around the world.	Asks deeper questions about God and about the child's own relationship to God. Begins to relate religious ideals to personal decision making. Begins to understand historical relationships and their significance for Christianity. Begins to determine own moral behavior in terms of knowledge of God as revealed in Christ. Expresses religious thoughts verbally. Begins to evaluate evidence and points of view and to arrive at own convictions. Begins to identify with the religious community and its work. Exploring meaning of commitment to God through Jesus Christ. Growing in understanding of value and responsibility of becoming a confirmed member of the church, and of the relationship of church membership to Christian commitment.

You are probably aware, through your illustrations, of the *uniqueness of each child.* Each child, as indicated at the beginning of the chart, is an individual person. Each has his or her own background, own environment, differing persons of importance in his or her life. Each has an individual personality, and his or her own ways of responding to people, things and situations. Each has his or her own particular capabilities and limitations. Out of all these influences, each child develops his or her own style of learning—a particular way of processing experiences and potential learnings.

Look again at the personal experience you described at the beginning of this chapter. Think of other anecdotes from your growing-up years and from recent years. Reflect on the interweaving of heritage, physical health, and relationships with other persons as factors in your learning experiences.

I offer two illustrations of my own:

1. Experiences of gaining self-confidence and strengthening of self-image through development of physical skills, with emotional as well as physical support from brothers and sister.

• at age 1½: my brother, age 3, holding one end of a stick for me to hold the other end as I tried beginning steps in walking; my brother gradually releasing his hold on the stick until I walked alone;

• about 7 years of age: older brother, about 10, letting me hold on to his shoulders so we could swim together until I could swim alone (weeks after my younger sister was swimming in deep water);

• at 8 or 9: sister, 15 months younger, steadying bicycle as I learned to balance it for riding by myself;

2. Experience of responding to and learning from two important persons in my life, with differing values in adult-child relationships and with differing ways of instructing/guiding the child in Christian growth—

Grandmother	Mother
• who came to live with us after my father's death when I was 10 years of age, and who still viewed mother as her child though an adult with family responsibilities	• who now had responsibilities previously carried by father, plus helping children adjust to new family group, of which grandmother was a part
• deep religious convictions, including definite ideas of rights and wrongs, with values often expressed in the tone of "thou shalt" or "thou shalt not"	• equally deep religious faith and commitment, including concerns for each child as a growing, developing child of God to be counseled in terms of guiding principles
• frequently answering child's "why" questions with "because I said so"	• usually answering "why" questions with point-of-view answers based on principles, time factors, or other reasoned or factual answers as appropriate to the situation

Factors in My Responses

• conscientiousness; timidity; fear of being wrong; low trust level in own capabilities, knowledge, judgments (e.g., in physical skills as illustrated above; in school work—my mother counseling me at third-grade level to try to give answers to teacher's questions in school even if not sure of being right);

• tendency to accept my grandmother's instructions as security of authority; seeking reassurances from my mother, who through the years had encouraged us children to make our own value decisions;

• need for further help then from my mother, and through the years from other persons, in realization that Christian living is not a matter of "do's" and "don'ts" but of determining and living by values rooted in one's heritage and in who one is as a responsible human being.

Some of our *concerns,* expressed in chapter 2, for children growing up in the 1970s and 1980s, pertain to young human beings in any era. Some particular concerns for children in this decade and the next are rooted in trends such as:

• living in an increasingly pluralistic society;

• rapidity of change in home, society, the world;

• increasing concern about the environment and the possibility of exhaustion of natural resources;

• unpredictability of the future.

Among other concerns in Christian education, relating to these trends, are increasing emphases on
• knowing the Bible as a goal, with "knowing the Bible" interpreted variously as

• knowledge, information about or from the Bible,

• understanding the message of the Bible,

• incorporating the meaning of that message in one's own life;

• development of values as another goal, with values seen as either or both of the following:

• rules and principles passed from one generation to another,

• personal beliefs and convictions that the individual affirms and lives by.

There are other goals in church education pertaining to the person's self-image as a child of God, his or her responses to God's love, heritage in the Christian faith, relationships with others of God's children and with the natural world. In chapters 1 and 2 we direct attention to more inclusive statements of objective and purposes of Christian education.

The *child in the church school* is continually dealing with how he or she will process potential learning experiences. Whatever the purposes and design of the teacher(s) for the teaching-learning situation, the child is faced with questions, choices, decisions of his or her own:

Who am I?

Why am I in this particular learning situation?

What will I do here?

Will I learn anything? What?

What will I do with what I learn?

A wide range of questions, verbalized or expressed in behavior, reflect varying degrees of child responsibility and concern for his or her own learning experiences.

Why am I here? What am I going to do?	Do I care about what is going on? Can I do anything about it?

Am I interested, uninterested, or
unconcerned about what is being taught?

Will I cooperate with the teacher(s)? Will I cooperate with the group? Am I responsible for what we do?	Does anyone care what I do?

How can I get anyone to pay attention to me?
To care what I am interested in?

How much freedom or restriction do I have in this situation? What am I going to do within those limits? Or how am I going to break out of the boundaries?	What do I want to learn? to explore? to do? Will my teacher(s) help me? Or do they have other ideas about what I should learn?

How am I going to choose what I want to do when I have the opportunity to select goals or activities? Are other children interested in the
same things? How can we work together? Or how can I work alone?

How do I carry out what I have chosen to do, or what I have been told by the teacher(s) to do?	How do I take the initiative, or cooperate with peer leaders, in group planning and activities?

How can I best use and develop my capabilities?
How can I overcome my limitations, handicaps? Or
use my limited abilities in constructive ways?

Each child's answers to her or his own questions come through in the ways that child behaves in the group as well as in how the child responds to content and procedures available to her or him.

In this chapter we examine different ways of learning related to kinds of decisions that are made by the learners, by the leaders, or by learners and leaders together. In the remainder of this chapter we see the child and his or her learning in relation to two content areas.

The content of Christian education comes from the concerns of the church, the faith community. Areas of concern are identified by the denominations separately or together and guidance for leaders in the local congregation is provided through church curriculum materials (see chapter 8). Teachers develop teaching procedures and use content in relation to what they consider important for the child and to the teachers' understanding of how learning happens.

For illustration, we use here thoughts on how children learn using two concerns of church leaders: how the child "learns the Bible" and how the child "learns values."

First, let's direct our attention to *how the child learns values.*[3]

What words, or ideas, come to your mind when we use the word "value" or speak of "values" being taught in Christian education? One group of responses to first thoughts on hearing the word "value" included: priority . . .commitment . . . preference . . . worth . . . significance . . . success . . . standards . . . ethics . . . meaning. To these spontaneous responses were added phrases such as

. . . anything that is important for any reason

. . . bases for determining one's course of action

THE LEARNER AND LEARNING

. . . preferential principle affirmed and used as
criterion in determining one's actions.[4]

Beliefs or points of view are indicators of values. They become values only when they are both affirmed and acted on in situations where the individual or group makes decisions based on those affirmed convictions.

A child learns from the reactions of others that some behavior is acceptable or unacceptable. As he or she begins to understand why such behavior is considered "right" or "wrong," "good" or "bad" the child begins to deal with values of those other persons as a base for determining his or her own values.

Children learn values as they
- experience making decisions;
- examine alternatives and possible consequences as bases for decision making;
- hear parents, teachers, others witnessing to their convictions and responding to "why" questions;
- observe adults, youth, and other children and become aware of consistency or inconsistency in those persons' value affirmations and their value-related behavior;
- deal with conflicting value systems (in home, peer group, from TV, community, elsewhere) and begin to take a personal stand in support of or independent of a position expressed by others.

Children in the church learn values and ways of making value decisions as they relate to church leaders, parents, and members of the congregation who
- witness to their beliefs, convictions;
- act in accord with their professed beliefs and their affirmation of God's love in their lives;
- involve children in simple choice-making situations as bases for later, more difficult decision making, using consideration of alternative possibilities and probable results of each;
- use verbalization as a means of interpreting valuing processes and affirming value positions;
- help children understand the enabling power of the Holy Spirit in the lives of persons—in making decisions and in fulfilling their commitments as disciples of Jesus Christ.

Learning of values and valuing procedures through church education is interrelated with the church's concerns for persons'
- response to the love of God;
- commitment to Christ;
- personal affirmation of beliefs, convictions (right-wrong, true-false, just-unjust, love-hate, faith or lack of faith in God, other valuing areas);
- individual and group actions expressing values rooted in Christian faith, beliefs, commitment.

Neither learning of values nor knowing the Bible is explicitly stated in the objective of Christian education. Both value development (values, valuing) and biblical literacy (knowledge, skills of use, understanding) are implicit in Christian education.

In thinking of *when the child learns the Bible,* we need to be clear in what we are concerned that the child learn.

Check one of the four ideas below indicating your own view of what is important for the child.

We want the child to learn

———what the Bible says—words, facts, what happened;

———what the meaning is of the verse, biblical event, or other information;

———what the message of the biblical passage is for the child's own life, what difference it makes for her or him in making decisions from day to day;

———all three of the above.

Children learn what the Bible says and gain information about the Bible through hearing the Bible read, memorizing selected verses, learning the two parts of the Bible (Old and New Testaments) and sections of the Bible (gospels, law, etc.), and through other ways of dealing with facts and content.

Children learn meanings as they
explore concepts of selected biblical passages.

Children learn the message of the Bible as they relate it to their own lives through dramatizing biblical stories and redramatizing the situations as present-day stories, as they examine situations in their own lives in light of the biblical message.

Children learn the significance of the Bible as a very important book as they have experiences with persons who find meaning in the Bible for their own lives.

The child's Bible learning, as well as other church school learning, is affected by her or his readiness for learning and what she or he is experiencing in the learning situation.

An eight-year-old first-grade boy in a two-class vacation school was placed in the older class because of the age-line division. This boy was noted in the community as a troublemaker. As teacher of the older class, I soon observed other boys teasing and picking on him to aggravate him into making a disturbance. I realized also that he did not have the reading ability for the kind of Bible study the group would be doing in exploring what it means to be a follower of Jesus. I ignored the horseplay among the boys. At play time I talked with the first-grader about what our class would be doing and what the other class was doing. I offered him the option of staying in our class or changing to the other class. His response was, "I'll go to the other class if you want me to go." I assured him I would be glad for him to stay in our class but thought he might enjoy the other class more. He could decide. We rejoined the group at play. A bit later he said, "I'd like to try the other class."

During conversation time in the younger children's class, this boy heard the teacher tell a story including a Bible verse. The teacher read the same verse from the Bible. The children talked about the verse, and the teacher read it again. The boy, now beginning to feel at home in the class, spoke up, "I can read that." Looking at the teacher's Bible he read the verse (from memory, after having heard it repeated several times).

At the end of the session he asked if he could take the Bible home to read to his parents. The teacher let him take her Bible. The next morning he came eagerly to me and the other teacher to report, "I read the Bible at home, and my mother and daddy read it too." (Later I learned that the minister of the church, knowing about this incident and the child's further involvement in the vacation-school experience, gave the boy a Bible of his own.)

Through this vacation-school experience this boy, with relational and reading difficulties, gained a new perception of himself as a person (accepted as himself, able to read from the Bible) and of the Bible (as a book he could use). His joyous report, "I read it and my mother and daddy read it too," was a triumphant affirmation.

Children and older persons have "four Bible-learning tasks":

> —experiencing the Bible content
> —discovering and expressing Bible meanings . . .
> —absorbing Bible backgrounds
> —acquiring Bible skills.[5]

"The Bible says to everyone, 'Here I am! In me there is the possibility of meaning for you! Discover it!'"[6] Boys and girls find genuine pleasure in learning to use their Bibles. They experience excitement and anticipation as the Bible becomes their own through skill development and through growth in understanding its message.

A minister, while reviewing the manuscript for this book, recalled a learning experience he had had with a group in a confirmation class some years ago. He asked the boys and girls to close their eyes and try to visualize what it would have been like to be in the crowd when Jesus said, "Let the children come!" After a few moments of serious thought one boy exclaimed, "I can see it in technicolor." The minister then asked, "Did the children go immediately when Jesus told the disciples and the crowd to let the children come to him." Several children quickly replied, "No!" When asked why, one responded, "They didn't go until Jesus looked at them." The minister, along with the boys and girls, gained new insight into the meaning of this very familiar passage.

When have children learned the Bible? They have learned
• when they have developed new skills in using the Bible,
• when they have gained new meanings,
• when they have increased in understandings of its implications for their own lives,
• when they have experienced and expressed biblical meanings in their own lives.

The children in the two illustrations were learning at the fact level: "I read the Bible," and "Jesus said, 'Let the children come.' " They were learning also at the meaning level: "The Bible is for me," and "The children came after Jesus looked at them." The confirmation class members dealt with the selected verse and other biblical passages in decision making at the valuing level. They asked themselves individually, "Do I want to commit my life to Jesus Christ, and to publicly affirm my commitment by becoming a full member of the church?"

Whatever the learning situation and content,
Each person has her or his own learning style

—a product of her or his own response
to self, to others;
to independence-dependence tendencies;
to various approaches in learning-teaching;
to leadings of the Holy Spirit;
to ways of organizing thoughts,
to past and present experiences in living-learning;
to ease or difficulty in using learning resources.

Each child, as well as older person, has a unique learning style, including
—ways of learning
• in which she or he is most responsive,
• in which she or he takes the initiative,
• in which she or he is involved in group goals and plans,
• in which the leader gives instructions;
—approaches in learning
• that are easiest,
• that are most comfortable,
• that are most interesting;
—approaches that are most effective for particular learning
• that may also be the easiest, or
• that may require struggle and effort in the learning.

Church education is most effective when each learner is enabled to use his or her strongest learning skills and is supported or guided in learning requiring other skills. The church is not in the business of teaching academic skills. Use of those skills, however, and skill enhancement for the individual are interwoven with developing self-concepts and with increasing ability to deal with concepts of the faith in relating to God, to others, to self.[7]

Other persons can provide and interpret information and can witness to their own faith in words and deeds, but the learner does his or her own learning as he or she
• deals with information, discovers meaning, makes the meaning his or her own;
• practices skills of relationships as well as mental and physical skills so that these become integral parts of the person's own actions;
• attains his or her own faith through experience of and response to God;
• assumes responsibility for his or her own life and actions as a child of God.

Chapter 5 continues our consideration of the learner and learning in different ways of learning and teaching.

WAYS OF LEARNING, WAYS OF TEACHING

''The preacher spoke hands with me!'' a young child reports with delight after a congregational service.

"I am important to God because I'm me!'' exclaims a five-year-old in a class of four- to eleven-year-olds exploring understanding of self.

A fifth-grade girl comes to one of her last year's fourth-grade teachers for comfort following a class

discussion of family relationships when her own parents
were in the process of completing divorce proceedings.

Christian education for the child comes primarily through involvement in the faith community:
Is the child accepted as "belonging" now in this church family? Or is she or he seen as a "future" church member? Does the child feel accepted in his or her own group, by youth and adults of the congregation? Does he or she feel recognized as a person of worth, a child of God, an active participant in the covenant community?

Does the child have opportunities to make decisions—alone or with others—in goal setting, active planning, developing class rules? What kinds of responsibilities is the child encouraged to assume and fulfill? How does she or he view self as a responsible (or irresponsible) member of the class or congregation? As needed or not needed in the life of the group? How are faith convictions of others shared with the child? Are his or her thoughts and feelings accepted by others? What interchange of developing understandings and of honest feelings is experienced?

Education of the child is taking place (positively or negatively) in all relationships within the congregation. All of the child's church experiences are the arena for Christian education. Within this broader learning arena, the church provides the church school for specific teaching-learning experiences.

Primary program goals of the church through Christian education include
• nurturing the child in the Christian faith
• instructing her or him in biblical heritage and in the heritage of the Christian church through the centuries
• involving her or him in the concerns of the church for ministry and mission.

In this chapter, we look at ways of organizing for the child's learning in church-school settings. For implications for children of a specific age we need to relate ideas here with ideas in chapter 4 on how children learn. Implementation of different ways of learning in teaching-learning experiences is further developed in chapter 6. Preparation for teaching alone or as a member of a teaching team is expanded on in chapter 9.

As you begin this examination of ways of learning, look at the chapter title, "Ways of Learning, Ways of Teaching." What are your expectations as you read that title? What comes to your mind as ways of learning and teaching? Check or add below your own thoughts:

_____ideas of various teaching-learning procedures such as drama, art, research;

_____thoughts of specific activities such as making puppets, painting pictures, finding information on specific
       topics;

_____experiences leading to a feeling of "I surely learned from that";

_____ways learners and teachers relate to each other in learning-teaching.

_____

In our overall exploration of learning and teaching we are concerned with all of these aspects of the learning experience.

In this book, I attempt to interpret learning and teaching in terms of
         • *ways* of learning and teaching,
         • *approaches* in church education,
         • *styles* of learning and teaching,
         • *methods* for learning.

Whatever word, phrase, or expression one chooses to symbolize a particular concept, that idea is further defined or clarified by the context in which the symbol is used. So that you may continue with me in our dialogue about church education, let's identify how I use the above phrases in this book. I invite your responses to concepts rather than to single words.

Ways of learning and teaching. How learners and leaders function in the learning situation; decision-making behavior; the degree and range of relationships of individual learners, group members, and teachers in determining what is to be learned or explored and how; relative quantity in making decisions—ratio, range, sphere, strength. (Interpreted in this chapter and in chapter 6.)

Approaches to learning in church education. Entry way for learning; covering canopy for the overall learning situation; means of access to learning experiences; general means or process of moving toward learning goals. (See chapter 10.)

Style of learning or teaching. A particular, distinctive, or characteristic manner of acting in the learning situation; one's general manner of entering into the learning experience—one's profile or silhouette as a learner or teacher. (See chapter 4 for learner characteristics; chapter 7 for teacher styles.)

Method for learning or teaching. A specific procedure or manner of working; an orderly, logical, or systematic way of instruction, inquiry, presentation; specific learning activity. (See pages 67-69 in chapter 9.)

We are concerned in this chapter with how we organize for children's learning experiences in the church school. One way of attempting to understand ways of learning-teaching is to examine what decisions are made in the learning situation and who makes what decisions.

THE BIG QUESTION

Who makes

What decisions

When

    -as learner

Why

    -as leader

How

How much *freedom* or *responsibility* does the learner have for
 • his or her own learning goals and efforts in working toward those goals,
 • working toward teacher-determined goals?
What decisions does the teacher make prior to the class session?
Why?
What decisions does the teacher expect the child to make?
In what situations are decisions made by the group—children and teacher(s) together?

When does a single *child* have the *right* to make his or her own decision? To what extent is he or she *accountable* for that decision? To whom is the teacher accountable for *teacher decisions?* What *administrative or policy decisions* of church officials affect working relationships of teacher(s) and class (individuals or group)?

Your answer to the last question above, will suggest for your own church the *boundaries within which teacher and class function.* Such boundaries usually include:
• age-range of class members
• room or space for class sessions
• teachers: one or more; ratio of teachers to number of children
• curriculum materials to be used
• amount of time available for class sessions.

Some congregations assume that the objective of Christian education and purposes indicated in the selected curriculum materials give adequate guidance for teachers as to that congregation's intentions through Christian education. Other congregations, through the education committee or commission or through the official policy-making body, provide a policy statement including goals of that congregation in its educational ministry. Such a statement includes expectations for teachers and other leaders in the educational program. The way in which the goals and expectations are stated and the seriousness with which these are viewed can be for teachers supportive or limiting.

Whatever support, guidance, counsel, enabling help, and limiting requirements the teacher receives, there are decisions for the teacher(s) to make. Basically, the teacher's decisions are rooted in answers to two questions:

1. What are the *role* and *responsibilities* of the *child* (children) in the learning experiences?

2. What are the *role* and *responsibilities* of the *teacher(s)* in relation to the learning experiences of the child (children)?

The way in which the teacher answers these two questions is a key to *how* that *teacher will function* in the learning situation. Teacher behavior (whether a single teacher or a teaching team) enables or inhibits the child in the degree of freedom or limits the child has in the learning setting.

Whatever the functioning relationships of learners and leaders (teachers), the *learner* is *responsible for processing his or her own learning.* Others may determine goals, guide procedures using selected resources and activities, and provide input of ideas or means of discovering insights. The value of all of these will be in proportion to their appropriateness for the individual learner in relation to his or her individual learning needs and readiness. Always, the individual is the only one who can process his own learning: making ideas or insights his or her own; working with skills until they are achieved; behaving in accord with, or contrary to, expressed values; responding in love (or hate) to other persons in the group and elsewhere; accepting the leadings of the Holy Spirit in his or her life.

In the following charts,[1] we focus on
• the way leaders and learners function in the learning situation,
• the way these persons organize facilities and resources for use in working toward learning goals.

THREE WAYS OF LEARNING

The learner in any learning situation does his/her own learning—minimal or maximum—in relation to
• own readiness for the intended learning
• individual capabilities and learning skills
• amount of appropriate leader or peer support and encouragement.

Teacher Directed Learning	Group Directed Learning	Self-directed Learning
Teacher or teaching team • determines goals • directs activities • provides and organizes resources Leader(s) may provide for • variety of activities for individual choice, small group selection, total group participation Teacher, teaching team, determines • schedule of activities • ways resources will be used • extent to which individuals or groups have freedom to choose activities Learners • participate as directed, cooperating in varying degrees • learn according to —individual readiness for the learning opportunities provided —own capabilities and interests Leaders evaluate • goal achievement • procedures • learner behavior	Teacher or teaching team guides the group in • determining group goals • making decisions about ways of working together • organizing resources for group use Leader(s) may provide • general framework within which group decisions are made —general area for exploration —basic resources —process for making group decisions Learners • make group decisions —setting own goals or modifying goals proposed by leader(s) —choosing activities and procedures for total group and for interest groups • may make individual choice of interest groups Leaders and learners together evaluate • goal achievement • group processes • working relationships in group	Teacher or teaching team serves as • facilitator • enabler • provider of resources. Leader(s) may provide, or involve learners in preparing, • learning areas with specific —learning goals —learning activities —resources • guides for individual —use of learning resources —in working toward own goals Each learner • chooses own learning goals • works at own pace • works alone, or with other persons as desired • interacts with leaders and other learners as he/she and they —discover and use resources —share ideas and experiences The learner, in consultation with a leader (leaders) evaluates • his/her own goal achievement • choice and pacing of activities • own relationships with others

The teacher (leader) or teaching team (leadership team) may
• use one of the above learning designs in determining extent to which leaders, learners, or leaders and learners together will develop learning goals and plans
• use a modification of one or more of these learning designs
• vary the learning design, according to anticipated need
—for leader input and process direction
—for building group relationships
—for individual pacing of learning.

TWO WAYS OF TEACHING

One teacher alone or a group of teachers may be responsible for
• guiding or enabling learners in securing information, discovering meanings, developing values
• determining plans for teacher directed, group directed, or self-directed learning.

Teaching Alone	Teaching With a Teaching Team
A teacher teaching alone has full responsibility for • making all leader preparation • deciding how he/she will work with the learners • relating to individual learners and to the group. A teacher teaching alone may secure counsel or assistance in teaching through • conferring with a counseling teacher or other educational supervisor • enlisting a parent(s), other person(s) in leadership for specific activities for a limited time • securing help from persons with specific skills in developing own skills or in guiding the group • requesting counseling teacher or someone else to observe in one session or longer for purpose of helping teacher evaluate the teaching-learning situation • participating in local/area leadership programs.	Teachers on a teaching team share responsibilities for • advance preparation • leadership role each will have in working with learners and ways learners will be involved • relating to individual learners and to the group. Teachers on a teaching team may assist each other through • taking responsibilities according to own skills and interests • helping each other in developing specific skills • supportive participation in planning and throughout sessions when someone else is in a leadership role. A teaching team may secure outside counsel or assistance in the same ways as an individual teacher • from other persons • through leadership enterprises.

WAYS OF MAKING LEARNING RESOURCES AVAILABLE TO LEARNERS

Resources for learning may be
- provided by leader(s) as leader(s) intends learners to use them
- available in a resource library or area for use there or for check out
- located in interest centers for use at designated times in session
- arranged in learning centers for self-directed use by learners.

A Resource Library or Area	Interest Centers	Learning Centers
A center for learning resources may be • a church resource library serving all church groups • a central resource area for one group or two or more groups. A resource center includes • books, other printed resources • art pieces, posters, objects • multi-media resources: films, filmstrips, records, tapes, kits • audio-visual equipment • work materials Resources, supplies and equipment are arranged for learners • to use in the library or area • to check out for individual or group use.	Usually used in teacher directed or group directed teaching-learning. Interest centers are set up • for use at designated times in a session • for activities related to overall learning goals. Interest centers may be used by small groups or individuals • for motivation of ideas or interest for total group planning • for study, exploration related to plans of total group • for expression of ideas or feelings. Learners are involved in total group planning and activities, including use of interest centers.	Usually used in self-directed learning situations. Each center, (learning center, learning station, learning area) • includes related resources • for use by individuals, alone or in groups • in pursuing goals for that area. Centers may be arranged by • themes, with resources, for exploration and self-expression • interest activities through which content is explored and ideas illustrated. Learners spend major time in centers working at own pace, with occasional together times.

Ways of learning and teaching as used in church education may be clearer against the background of an interpretation of "Three Modes of Teaching" found in *Teaching Toward Inquiry,* Schools for the 70's Series.[2] The three modes of teaching there described are identified as: lecturing, or *didache* teaching; socratic teaching; and inquiry teaching. The description of each mode includes: what the teaching mode is, the teacher's role, how input is handled, and the basis for evaluation.

Lecture or didache teaching is a telling, assignment-giving, describing technique. This mode of teaching is functional in passing on information. The teacher decides what should be presented to the class and how it will be presented. Didache teaching is intended to provide input. It is one way of communicating information from the teacher to the student. The teacher selects the material to be presented and encourages the student to attend to it. The student's role in didactic teaching usually involves receiving and storing the input. Evaluation is based on the student's ability to retrieve information from his storage without acting on that information to transform it in any way.

Socratic teaching is essentially a question-asking technique. It is one kind of programmed learning. Certain valued ends are best achieved with this mode of teaching. The teacher decides what questions to ask of the students. Like didactic teaching, Socratic teaching is intended to provide input. The teacher selects the material to be presented and encourages the student to attend to it. In this mode of teaching, however, the teacher's questions lead the student through additional kinds of intellectual operations: storing, processing, and output. Learning to "do" these operations himself is a bonus by-product for the student. Evaluation is based on the student's ability to recall information that has been somewhat transformed as a result of his and the teacher's intellectual efforts.

Inquiry teaching is directed toward the development of students who are more autonomous in initiating and directing their own learning. A transfer of learning occurs, assisting children in solving problems they meet in the real world. The teacher's role is complex. He (she) must analyze the student's present level of development and employ behaviors that will facilitate the student's growth from that point forward. In teaching toward inquiry, the teacher intends that the student learn how to decide what input he needs, what he should store, how it should be stored, and when and what kinds of processing should be done on what kinds of data or ideas. In other words, teaching toward inquiry is intended to help a student learn how and when to use the range of intellectual processes. In this mode of teaching, the student finds his own way through these processes. The instructional goal is clearly one of process learning: the development of students who are more autonomous learners. Evaluation is based on the student's ability to apply these processes to the next problem.[3]

The three ways of learning in church education, as charted on page 35, are: teacher-directed learning, group-directed learning, and self-directed learning. Below we see these three ways of learning as they relate to the three modes of teaching described above.

Teacher-directed learning, as it is seen in church education, includes both *didache* teaching and Socratic teaching. Teachers provide input (using Bible passages, stories, other resources), give step-by-step instructions including individual or group assignments, ask questions. The child is expected to receive and store information, to give back information (memorized Bible verses, answers to questions) as it was given or to answer questions with answers processed by the child. Evaluation is based on the child's ability to retrieve information according to the teacher's expectations (information as given by teacher or as processed by child).

Group-directed learning, as observed in church education, is an adaptation of inquiry teaching with focus on group inquiry and relationships within the group as the major means of learning. Teachers guide group process and make available resources for group use. The child, along with other members of the group, is working simultaneously on processing data from inquiry (as conducted by the individual, small group, or total group) and data from his or her own experiences as a group member. Evaluation is based on group goal achievement and on ability of group members to use data out of inquiry and group process.

Self-directed learning, as viewed in church education, is inquiry teaching with focus on individual inquiry, with each child assuming initiative in his or her own explorations. Relationships develop as learners work side by side or choose to work together. Teachers serve as enablers, facilitators, supporters, counselors, for individual children. Each child directs his or her own plan of inquiry and processes data from that inquiry for personal use or for sharing with the group. Evaluation is based on individual goal achievement and on ability of individuals to process and use data from inquiry and their own working procedures and relationships.

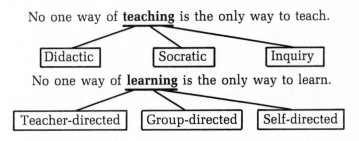

No one way of **teaching** is the only way to teach.

| Didactic | Socratic | Inquiry |

No one way of **learning** is the only way to learn.

| Teacher-directed | Group-directed | Self-directed |

Each of these ways of teaching and of learning has value when used appropriately. Any one of these used exclusively limits the range and possibilities for some kinds of learning. Didactic and Socratic teaching and teacher-directed learning focus more in intellectual learning from data input. There is minimal, if any, attention to learning through relationships or through inquiry-discovery. Inquiry teaching as used in group-directed learning involves the learner in relationships and inquiry. The individual experiences learning how to live and work with others while processing data. Personal learning needs are often sublimated if these differ from the group needs. Inquiry teaching in self-directed learning provides the learner opportunity to pursue personal goals and interests. The child may miss some of the values of teacher input and group relationships unless the individual child chooses to seek the resources that teacher and fellow-learners can provide.

The teacher, or teaching team, may provide opportunities for learning which include teacher input, group process, and personal inquiry. Each teacher or teaching team may:
• vary teaching-learning designs according to goal-related needs for leader input and process direction, for building group relationships, or for individual pacing of learning,
• begin with one of the three ways of learning and teaching, making adaptations for meeting other special individual or group needs.

For most persons, learning takes place in various ways:
• through self-direction (spontaneous, self-initiated, self-paced);
• through directions from others (parent, teacher, friend, someone else);
• through group direction (group process of family, peer group, club, class).
No one of these ways of learning is the only way. Learning at times is more effective
• with individual initiation and action with reflection on the learning experience;
• with group planning and implementation in seeking information or working on a group-selected project;
• with leader (teacher or other leader) guidance or direction including leader input, instruction, and/or process direction.

Seldom are all decisions in the church-school class made exclusively by teacher, group, or individual child. Learning in the church school is seen as self-directed, group-directed, or teacher-directed in terms of *who makes the major decisions* in the learning process—that is, who has the greatest influence in ratio, range, sphere, strength, and extent of decisions
in goal setting,
in determining approaches in learning,
in use of activities and resources for learning,
and in evaluating progress
toward goal achievement.

In summary, the roles and responsibilities of teacher(s) and child(ren) in the three ways of learning may be characterized as indicated below.

Teacher-directed learning
• action centered in teacher input and child response;
• teacher input of content, concepts, values, step-by-step procedures: teacher telling, giving information, making assignments to individuals or small groups;
• child response in answering teacher's questions (usually when called on by teacher), following teacher's directions;
• teacher(s) responsible for discipline, children cooperating or reacting negatively to teacher directives;
• teacher plans include step-by-step content presentation and/or activity instructions;
• child decision making in terms of what he or she will do with teacher input and directions.

Group-directed learning
• action spread among group members, including teacher(s): inquiry, research, discovery, sharing as input for fellow group members;
• input provided by both teacher(s) and children, particularly in procedural plans, but also in content information and ideas on concepts and values;
• group responsibility in discipline—in defining rules, limits, freedoms;
• teacher guidance in group decision making and action—in process, in helping group members identify possible alternatives both in rule setting and in enforcement of rules;
• teacher plans include procedures for involving the group members in making group decisions about own plans and activities;

- individual learner processes his or her own attitudes toward co-learners and leader(s) as they work together; determines how and to what extent he or she will accept the findings of the group in its study explorations.

Self-directed learning
- individual action, self-direction in exploration in relation to own goals (defined by individual or selected from goals proposed by the teacher or teaching team);
- input gained primarily from selected resources and research procedures provided by teacher(s) or developed by individuals or the group;
- interaction among children and between children and teacher(s) as children work in learning areas, use resources together, choose to work together on common goals, activities, projects,
- self-discipline more characteristic owing to freedom of choice in working procedures;
- teacher serves as counselor, facilitator, provider of resources, enabler of learner(s), who makes own decisions about goals, procedures, activities;
- teacher plans include collecting of resources and developing guidance for individuals to use in determining own learning activities and in using those activities in working toward selected goals;
- individual decision making in regard to use of one's own time and efforts during the session as well as how he or she will make use of his or her own findings.

Whatever way of teaching each of us uses, we are concerned with *the child's spiritual growth* within the total life development of the child.

Stop and consider. What is meant by the spiritual life of a person? How does a child mature in "faith, hope, and love"? . . .

The spiritual life of a person, young or old, involves his [or her] deep inner feelings—feelings about [self], about one's fellow beings, about God. It involves . . . responses to God, [to Jesus Christ and to the Holy Spirit. It involves also responses] to other persons, [and to the natural world. These responses may be] spontaneous or reasoned.

Observe children—infants, toddlers, run-abouts, school agers. Become aware of situations, experiences, persons to which they respond. Note how they show or express their response through physical or emotional reaching out or withdrawal. Try to sense what they are feeling: love, anger, fear, trust, hope, despair, other emotions. Attempt to identify what these experiences mean to children (not what adults think should be, but specific children's own meanings).

Explore ways children discover, learn, develop . . .
- perceptions of themselves, who they are;
- ideas, insights about God, responsiveness to God;
- attitudes toward other persons, relationships with them.

Remember that children learn in many ways:
- primarily through their own daily experiences,
- through observation of other persons and imitation of their behaviors, and
- through identification and interpretation of feelings and actions—their own and those of other persons.

Note ways teachers, parents, the congregation can
- encourage and support children in their spontaneous "childlike" faith;
- help children, at their own level of understanding, to identify what they are observing or feeling about God and his creations—the universe, other persons, themselves;
- help children grow from simple identification of the Bible as a special book in early years to increasing realization of the meaning of the biblical message;
- enable older children to see themselves (as well as biblical persons and writers) as searching for and responding to God and his will for their lives;
- enable children to express verbally and nonverbally their positive responses to God and to other persons and to cope with their negative feelings in constructive ways;
- enable children to make responsible choice decisions in regard to their own day-by-day actions and attitudes, as they reach a level of maturity when they can understand possible consequences of alternative decisions. (At first simple "yes-no," "I want—I don't want" reactions to specific situations. Later more generalized "I ought—I ought not," "I will—I will not");
- enter into experiences of fellowship with children in recognizing God's plan for life, for love, for trust and hope, and in expressing to God true feelings of trust, hope, joy, anticipation, and also of fear, uncertainty, repentance.[4]

In chapter 6 we continue our exploration of the teacher's roles and responsibilities in the child's church-school learning experiences.

THE TEACHER AND TEACHING

"I know I'm right because
that is what my teacher said."
—an early elementary child.

"This is the teacher
who loves me! "—a
kindergarten child.

The teacher is one who instructs / guides / directs
in a particular class or group in
the church school.

I am aware of the concerns of many church educators whether "teacher" or "leader" best identifies the person working with a group of children (or youth or adults) in church education.

For some persons:

Leader is one who guides, leads, enables persons in learning.

Teacher is one who imparts, instructs, passes on knowledge.

For others:

Teacher is one who has directing/guiding responsibilities in the teaching-learning setting.

Leader is anyone with leadership responsibility (administrators, committee chairpersons, officers, teachers).

I am aware also of a problem of using either "teacher" or "leader" for identifying this designated job. Teachers and children are all both leaders and learners, teachers and persons taught. All are members of the group with varying roles and responsibilities. In the confirmation-class illustration (page 31) the children became teachers for the minister. He still remained the designated teacher or leader.

For our purposes, I have chosen to use the term "teacher." This is the identity most often used for the person assigned the leadership role in a teaching-learning group. The teacher, to me, is a co-learner with other group members and in addition has a special role and responsibility in the group.

How do you see the teacher? Check the idea below that best describes role of a teacher, or write your own statement.

_____The teacher is one who instructs the child, with the teacher determining goals and directing learning procedures.

_____The teacher is one who sets learning goals in terms of child needs and involves the child in determining learning procedures.

_____The teacher is one who guides the child, or group of children, in setting learning goals and deciding procedures for working toward those goals.

_____The teacher is one who is aware of child needs, interests, and capabilities and determines extent to which the child can and will be involved in determining learning goals and procedures.

_____

I see teaching as giving instruction where this is needed, and also as guiding persons in inquiry-discovery learning. I see the *teacher*, then, as *one who shares her or his own faith, understandings, insights in a way that encourages/challenges/supports other learners in their developing understandings of God's love and will for them, responsiveness to the Holy Spirit in their own search for meaning in life, developing values as persons responsible for their own learning and actions.*

In our effort to clarify our perceptions of roles and responsibilities of teachers, two primary resources are our experiences of others as teachers and our view of ourselves as teachers. Use number 1 below for recalling three teachers you have known. Use number 2 for describing yourself as teacher.

1. Divide a sheet of paper in three columns. At the top of each column write the name of a teacher whom you recall from your childhood.

First teacher:	Second teacher:	Third teacher:

Quickly write brief statements, words, or phrases which help you to sharpen your memory of each teacher. After making the three lists, look back over what you have written. What kinds of ideas did you record? Were these similar for the three persons? Or were characteristics of the three teachers quite different?

2. Make a similar three-column list for thinking of yourself as teacher. Put your own name at the top of each column. Below your name in each column write the name of a child in your class (or other group with which you are related). Use your imagination, based on experiences you have had with each of the three children, to list how you think each child might describe you. Again, look back over your lists. How similar, or different, are the ideas in the three columns?

Teacher's name: Child's name:	Teacher's name: Child's name:	Teacher's name: Child's name:

Keep your two three-column lists for reference as you work with styles of teaching (chapter 7). For now, you might find it interesting and useful to write your own statement describing an ideal teacher. Use selected ideas from your two lists and add other thoughts that now occur to you.

The ideal teacher:———————————————————————

———————————————————————

In all probability, no one teacher—yourself or anyone else—would measure up to your ideal for a teacher. Each of us has limitations as well as capabilities in skills and relationships. Each of us is conscious of expectations of church-school administrators, parents, congregation, and children in regard to what is to be taught and how. Time for teaching is limited. Facilities and resources provided or available may be adequate or short of what we feel is needed. The children's learning styles and their capabilities and limitations affect our ways of teaching.

Each of us can, on the other hand, build on our own strengths. We can seek assistance in teaching (co-teachers with strengths where we are weak, helpers for specific teaching tasks for which we feel inadequate). Because of who you are and what your understanding of teaching is, you may find teaching with a team of teachers to be desirable, or you may prefer to teach alone. (See chart on pages 35-36).

In *teaching in the church school,* the overall guide to what is to be taught and how is the *objective* of the church in Christian education (page 10). In brief, that objective is that all persons be aware of and respond to God's love, and that they live in faith and love. In each curriculum unit for church-school classes, there are suggested goals that teachers may accept, adapt, or revise. In between the general objective and these quite specific goals, the teacher or teaching team has some general purposes in teaching. (See chapter 2 for historical and current church statements of aims, purposes, goals, objectives.)

The following statements may help in clarifying your own overall intentions in teaching children in the school of the church. First, read through the series of ideas. On the left write yes by each thought you feel is valid. Write no by any idea you would reject as a teacher.

Next, be a bit more specific. Of the purpose statements you marked yes, which seems most important to you? Put the number 1 to the right of that statement. Put 2 and 3 by the second- and third-rank statements of purpose. In the same way, rank the statements of concern and of reason for teacher planning. Do not give a rank to any idea marked no on the left.

My *purpose* in teaching in the church school is

——— that children may learn content: knowing certain biblical passages (23rd Psalm, Beatitudes, Lord's Prayer, others); giving right answers to questions about the Bible, God, Jesus, and to questions about right behavior; ———

——— that children may understand concepts: understanding the message of the Bible (what was happening and why in different situations); what happened and why in church history; identification of parallel situations in church and society today and also in personal life; ———

——— that children may develop values: exploring biblical message, church history, present happenings in terms of what the child would have done in the situation and why, what experiences he or she has for which the biblical message or other content has meaning; what beliefs and concepts he or she feels important for his or her own decision-making and living. ———

My *concern* in teaching is with

——— teaching the lesson as a specific body of knowledge (story, biblical passage, information about the church, rules for Christian living, etc.) so that the children will be knowledgeable about the Bible and the tenets of the Christian faith; ———

——— teaching the curriculum unit to children following carefully the guidance of the writer, so that the children may have a well balanced experience in Christian education as outlined by curriculum developers; ———

——— teaching children through bringing together their experiences and the gospel message—using resources from happenings in the class group, from children's recall of day-by-day experiences, and from curriculum materials and other print and multi-media materials including the Bible. ———

My *reason* for preliminary planning is that I may more effectively

——— instruct children in knowledge and use of the Bible and in ways of right living; ———

——— guide children in group process so that they may learn through interaction with one another and with the teacher(s) as they explore ideas available through the Bible, their church school materials, and other resources; ———

——— enable individual children or the group in inquiry-discovery learning, using not only the Bible and student book, but also other resources—persons, print, multi-media, the church community, the world. ———

If you are on a teaching team, a comparison answers to the above by the individual teachers will help you see to what extent your team members are together in your teaching intentions. Differing reactions are to be expected, for each teacher is a person with her or his own background of experience and own views. Differences will suggest points at which teachers on a team may want to explore how they can come to a common view or how they can attain unity with divergent views.

Your ranking of the above ideas will provide some clues for the way of teaching you would find preferable or most comfortable. (See ways of teaching in chapter 5.) In any given teaching-learning situation

• few, if any, of us would determine our way of teaching entirely in terms of what would be most comfortable or easiest for the teacher(s);

• few, if any, of us would use strictly one way of teaching or another (teacher-directed, group-directed, self-directed);

• most of us would make some adaptation of one of these ways in order to meet specific needs of individual children or the group; or would vary our way of teaching from time to time in relation to immediate goals.

The *teacher's or teaching team's plan* for working with a class reflects:

• teacher knowledge about children in general—their needs, their interests, how they learn;

• teacher knowledge of individual children in her or his own group—capabilities, limitations, concerns, interests;

• teacher ideas on guidance of individuals or groups in self-understanding and self-determination and/or in teacher direction;

- teacher understanding of the faith, the heritage, and what message should be communicated with or to the learner;
- where the teacher intends to begin in bringing the learner and the gospel message together (Bible applied to life; life experiences with related biblical message; point of intersection of gospel message and life);[1]
- teacher acceptance, adaptation, revision of curriculum statements of goals, content, procedures;
- teacher (or teaching team) perception of roles of learner, group, and leader(s) in planning, in implementing plans, in evaluating progress;
- teacher perception of learning as knowing, being and/or doing. (See chapter 1.)

Adaptations for learners to make some decisions can be made in any of the three ways of teaching. Whether the major learning goals and teaching-learning plan are determined by teacher(s) or by group members, there may be:
- project committees (projects previously determined by teacher or group) with committee members clarifying
  —goal for the specific project (research information, product, action),
  —reason for project (why it is desired),
  —process for the project (how work is to be done),
  —evaluation (how to know when the project has been completed to the group's satisfaction);
- activity centers with individual choice of preferred activity (drama, art, music, research, Bible study, etc.);
- interest groups, with
  —individual choice of work group,
  —group decision for procedure (ways of working) in own group,
  —group and/or individual responsibility for carrying out various actions in the group plan.

There are varying degrees of teacher, child, and group decision according to the teacher's design as to which way of learning is dominant.
- In teacher-directed learning
  —the teacher(s) will likely determine what each project, activity, or interest group is to be,
  —perhaps allowing each child to choose where he or she will work,
  —with the teacher(s) providing instructions for each group or allowing group members or individuals to develop plans within designated boundaries,
- In group-directed learning
  —the teacher(s) will likely guide the group in selecting a project, determining what interest groups will contribute to the total group plan,
  —perhaps necessitating teacher guidance in negotiating individual differences of opinion or in finding ways of allowing for individual deviation from group plans,
- In self-directed learning
  —the teacher(s) will likely counsel with individuals about their interests or allow them to choose from among possibilities provided through learning centers;
  —possibly, the teacher would help individuals to locate other children interested in working on the same project so that they might form their own committee for their self-initiated project.

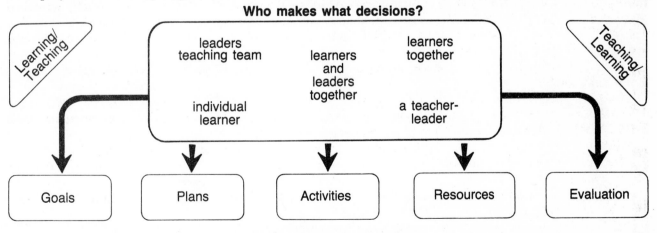

Who makes what decisions?

Learning/Teaching

leaders teaching team

learners and leaders together

learners together

individual learner

a teacher-leader

Teaching/Learning

Goals Plans Activities Resources Evaluation

Teachers, or teachers and learners together, can be *creative in* designing plans for teaching-learning experiences. In the following charts we seek to clarify how teachers develop and implement plans in different ways of learning-teaching. We show some of the steps teachers take in planning, teaching, and evaluating.

This chart may be used in two ways:

1. for planning and teaching creatively, using one of the ways of learning as the basic design, read down one column;

2. for comparison of various steps in the three ways of learning, read across the page, section by section.

The Creative Teacher or Teaching Team

In Teacher-Directed Learning	In Group-Directed Learning	In Self-Directed Learning
Considers individual needs, how to deal with these in total group and/or in interest groups, what resources are needed.	Considers how to guide group in group planning and in including individual interests in plans, how to guide group in securing resources, what stimuli are needed to help group set learning direction.	Considers how to allow for individual differences (needs, interests) in provision of environment and resources for child pursuit of own learning.
Develops set of goals (teacher determined or adapted from curriculum guide) to be achieved by individuals or group.	Develops list of possible goals for consideration by group and/or procedure for group development of goals.	Develops alternate goals from which individuals may select, or a plan for enabling each child in stating his or her own goals.
Adapts activity suggestions in curriculum unit, adds or substitutes own ideas in light of own perception of student needs, interests, capabilities.	Adapts activity suggestions, offering ideas from lesson writer and teacher to group for consideration along with ideas of group members.	Adapts activity suggestions, developing guides for individual use based on unit writer's ideas/teacher's ideas/children's ideas; or works with learners in determining own learning guides and directions.
Prepares teaching plan including goals, procedures, resources.	Prepares plan for guiding group in developing goals and procedures and in selecting resources.	Prepares plan for learning areas (centers, stations) with identified goals, resources, and guides for individual use.
Plans for stimulating participation and response in the total group; guiding choice when alternate activities or interest groups are provided; giving direction for learner participation in total and small group activities.	Plans for guiding the group in assessing alternate goals and/or activity choices, making group decisions, working as a total group or dividing for small group work toward class goals.	Plans for facilitating individual decision making in goal setting or selection, in selecting learning area (content/activity), in developing discovery procedures and/or following instructions in learning areas or programmed guides.
Provides for decision making by learners through committee work, choice of interest group, individual activities calling for creativity in planning and implementation.	Provides for decision making by learners through process of group goal setting, planning, evaluating; with some allowance for individual choice as to how child intends to contribute to achievement of group goals.	Provides for decision making by learners through programmed guides with alternate steps; individual pacing in work; use of learning centers with individual freedom in goal selection, areas for exploration/expression/study.

Provides for involving learners in problem-solving experiences: finding/affirming right answers under teacher guidance; identifying similar personal or group problems and suggesting appropriate behavior responses.

Provides for involving learners in problem-solving experiences: participating in group consideration of alternative solutions and in group conclusions as to preferred solutions.

Provides for involving learners in problem-solving experiences: making individual judgments of right answers in light of exploration of factors involved, or determining preferred solution from among alternatives after considering possible consequences of each.

Provides for exchange of ideas, insights, products: inviting members of group to share ways individuals have applied data from previous session(s) in through-the-week experiences.

Provides for exchange of ideas, insights, products: guiding group members in looking together at alternate ways of problem solving; sharing ideas and research data for use in reaching group conclusions for dealing with problems or for developing further insights.

Provides for exchange of ideas, insights, products: encouraging individuals to seek help (from other children or teachers) in finding needed resources, to invite other learners to cooperative inquiry and to share findings from individual or collective exploration.

Plans for learner involvement in evaluation: using feedback questionnaires or verbal response to questions relating to (a) information retrieval, (b) procedure preferences.

Plans for learner involvement in evaluation: using procedures for group self-assessment in (a) group goal achievement, (b) group process, and (c) ways of meeting individual needs.

Plans for learner involvement in evaluation: guiding each child in self-assessment of (a) personal goal achievement, (b) own work procedures, and (c) extent to which individual worked with others or hindered others in their work.

Considers need for other ways of learning: looking for points at which provision can be included for individual choice of activities or for group decisions.

Considers need for other ways of learning: guiding group in finding ways to incorporate individual interests, concerns and ways to allow for individual input in group data gathering.

Considers need for other ways of learning: finding ways of providing for interaction among learners, group relationships, experiences of cooperative decision making.

Takes account of questions such as: how to provide for individual capabilities, interests, needs within teacher plan; how to bring absentees up to date without using undue time of other learners in review.

Takes account of questions such as: how to allow for individual choice within the group plan; what is role of the leader (teacher) in group planning.

Takes account of questions such as: how to give instructions for individual use by children with reading difficulties; how much freedom, independence children are ready for; how to provide guidance for children needing support, supervision.

A teacher or teaching team continually rediscovers that *every child has special needs* in the sense that each child is different from every other child. Some individual needs can be met through the planning steps outlined in the chart on the previous pages. Some needs call for special planning.[2]

One key to meeting individual needs is to have enough adult leaders to make it possible to give time to individual children. With two or more teachers working together, one teacher can more easily work with a child having a particular relational or learning difficulty.

Some teachers, teaching alone, find ways for giving personal attention to each child, within the session or at some other time. In some cases, a teacher alone would be unable to work with the rest of the class while providing special support or guidance needed by a particular child. At times this teacher would need to arrange for a helper to come into the class or to make some arrangement for the child outside the class.

Some individual needs that call for special planning are identified below with notes on suggested relationship of the leader to the child.

The emotionally disturbed child. Any child may occasionally have an off day due to illness, an upset at home, overactivity during the week. He or she may need extra love and attention from a teacher or some quiet activity alone rather than group involvement. A mildly emotionally unstable child may be helped by an understanding teacher-friend to control his or her own behavior and to relate acceptably in the group. A child with problems serious enough to be identified as emotionally disturbed needs out-of-class family and professional help.

The slow child. The child who has difficulty keeping up in class activities needs alternative activities and/or freedom to work at his or her own pace. The teacher(s), aware of varying interests and work pace, may choose from a variety of activities in student and teacher books. Include one or more easy activities each session. If you have a teaching team, one teacher may give special help to a child needing assistance with reading, writing, artwork, etc.

The accelerated child. Adult-child conversation is important to discover individual interests and skills. Leaders determine where a child is in his learning and suggest new experiences. In a one teacher leadership situation, an accelerated child may assist the adult in some of the leadership functions. Special assignments may be used by the accelerated child—selected from activities suggested in teacher or student books.

For additional books and other resources to share with the accelerated child, see resources listed in *Planbook for Leaders of Children,* revised annually (Nashville: Graded Press).

The mentally retarded child. Some mentally retarded children are able to learn in an average class in the church school with individual help. If other handicapping conditions exist, such as paralysis, hearing loss, or limited sight, an additional leader may be needed to give major attention to this one child. If the mental retardation is severe, an additional leader or a separate class for the mentally retarded is indicated.

The blind child. A blind child without other handicapping conditions is a normal child who can't see. This child can do anything the other children do except read, write, and look at pictures. Leaders may record on cassette tape stories, including Bible material, music, and discussion questions (obtaining copyright permission when necessary). Sighted children soon learn to be "eyes" for the blind child. Through these experiences the sighted child learns compassion and the blind child is included in the class learning experiences.

The hearing impaired child. Considerable skill is required of the leader in ministering to a child with a hearing loss. Leaders should keep in close touch with parents in order to keep abreast of what hearing and speech therapists are recommending for methods of communication with the child. Psychological problems of frustration, withdrawal, and aggressiveness often are present. An extra adult to help the hearing impaired will strengthen communication. A child with a hearing loss may be slower in acquiring reading skills than children with hearing. Try using story papers, books, and even study books for the age group just younger than the age of the child you are working with.

As a single teacher or a teaching team works with a group of children (or other group), that teacher or team develops or creates a unique style of teaching. The teacher or team determines a basic way of relating to and working with children as a group and as individuals. The teacher or team determines how to work with individual or group needs, interests, capabilities, limitations. The teaching team decides how to function as a team in planning, in working with the children, and in evaluation and teacher growth.

In chapter 7 you are invited to participate in a process of identifying characteristics of your present teaching style, and changes you would like to make as an individual teacher or as a teaching team.

PLANNING FOR TEACHING AND LEARNING IN YOUR CHURCH

SECTION III

INVENTING YOUR OWN STYLE OF TEACHING

You are the teacher, or member of a teaching team of two or
more persons.
What is your present teaching style?
How satisfied are you with your style—your
ways of relating to other leaders and learners,
ways or organizing for teaching and learning?
What changes would you like to make in your ways of teaching?
How will you initiate and implement change?

Look at teaching-learning experiences, in which you serve as leader, as though you were viewing a drama. Just step back and visualize your own teaching-learning situation as an unfolding drama.

The Title: "The Drama of Learning and Teaching"

Point of view: Your own. The producers, characters, and scenes are as you see them. Notes below may help you visualize your drama.

Background: Your own experiences in learning and teaching. Your own understandings of what learning is: experiential learning, directed learning; and what teaching is: roles, responsibilities of learners, leaders.

The Setting: Formal staging for planned action.
Theater in the round for anticipated spontaneous action.

The child: Audience, participant, or central character (passive listener, reactor, responder, active participant; following teacher-direction, group-direction, self-direction).

The teacher: Director, central character, or supporting character (monologist, dialogist, puppeteer, property manager, director, or participant in spontaneous interaction).

Drama guide: Curriculum resources; used as
• script (to be learned or followed by teacher and class), or
• clues for action (source of content with ideas for methods of proceeding)

Sponsor: The local congregation or cooperating local churches, with the backing of the denomination or cooperating denominations.

Stage-manager–producer: The education committee through the education chairperson or church-school superintendent. (Or perhaps these become sponsors on behalf of the congregation, leaving entire stage management–production to teacher-director.)

Props managers: For facilities and equipment—the building committee; for curriculum materials—the education committee and literature secretary; for special supplies—teachers, education committee, or supply committee or secretary.

Synopsis: A brief summary of the "Drama of Learning and Teaching" as you see it in action in your class.

Now, back to your own style of directing, guiding, or enabling children in learning; to your own ways of interacting with children and other teachers in learning-teaching together.

Learning / teaching is not a drama with actors and directors. It is real. But there is drama in learning and teaching. Both students and teachers take many roles: as initiators of learning, enablers of other learners, stimulators of ideas, providers of resources, implementers of group or individual plans, seekers of knowledge or solutions to problems, discoverors of insights, givers and receivers of information, and so on.

Style of teaching is a *combination of* the *teacher's attitudes, actions* and *relationships* in the teaching-learning situation. It includes
- the teacher's attitudes toward self as leader and toward role of leader (one who instructs, informs, or guides learners);
- the teacher's attitudes toward the child (or other person) as learner (as a person to be taught by a teacher "who knows" or as a co-learner with other group members including the teacher who has special contributions to make from personal experience and preparation);
- the teacher's actions related to understanding of what is most important for the child to learn/experience/assimilate, and how the child can be taught/involved in learning;
- the teacher's ways of affirming and supporting, or dehumanizing, the child as a person.

You, as a single teacher or as a member of a teaching team, possess, create, invent your own teaching style. Your style is an outgrowth of your own
- point of view on ways of learning;
- understanding of the persons you teach—as members of the learning group and as individuals;
- concepts of what teaching is and of the learning-teaching experience;
- realization of your own skills, possibilities, limitations as director or guide of teaching-learning;
- principles for guiding your relationships with the learners.

We have used one art form (drama) to help you look at your own teaching style more objectively. Now, try another art form (drawing word pictures) for portraying your individual teaching style as it is and as it might become.

Think of *your teaching style* as a profile portraying features of the way you function in the teaching-learning experience with your class. View your profile from the angle of self-perception. Include thoughts on what you feel other persons expect of you (children, parents, administrators, congregation), for these affect your perception of yourself.

In the following exercises you are drawing your profile as a teacher: the general form, shape, contour, or picture in basic outline. Your teaching style will vary a bit from time to time, just as physical features sometimes change shape with a smile, a frown, a quizzical expression. You can, however, outline your most prominent features which give characterization to your teaching style.

You are your own artist. So draw a word profile of yourself as teacher. Show present features in your teacher profile. Think about changes you would like to make as you explore further your role and relationships as a teacher and as you have additional experience in teaching.

The only "right" answers for you are those which most nearly represent your view of yourself as teacher or member of a teaching team. If you are on a teaching team, you might want to use these exercises in one of the following ways:
(a) each teacher drawing his or her own profile;
(b) each teacher sharing personal profile with others on the team, inviting reactions in terms of how other team members experience or observe that teacher;
(c) team members together drawing a composite team profile;
(d) individual team members drawing profile of the teaching team then comparing these perceptions.

Remember, all answers are your own. Add qualifying phrases where clarification is needed before you can check statements. Be fair and honest with yourself. Affirm your strong points, and acknowledge limitations or need for change. Only with such openness can these exercises provide an adequate self-portrait and become a basis for reshaping your profile to the form you would prefer. Use "I" for yourself as teacher, or substitute "we" if you are drawing a team profile.

THE SETTING IN WHICH I TEACH

(Your profile is placed against the backdrop of your own teaching situation: persons in your class; helps/limitations/resources provided by your church; the setting in which you teach.)

1. The *setting.*
   a. The *children* I (we) teach are: age(s) ———, grade(s) ———, with (number)——— in class and average attendance of ———.
   b. Our class *space or room* is (front corner of sanctuary, classroom on third floor, or . . .)——————— .
   c. Our basic equipment for the class includes:———————————————————— .
   In addition we have access to———————————————————————— .
   d. The teacher or teaching team can best be identified as:
   ——— one teacher teaching alone;
   ——— a teaching team with a lead teacher and one or more helpers or assistants;
   ——— a teaching team of two or more teachers who share responsibilities in planning, teaching, and evaluation, with one teacher as team chairperson or coordinator;
   ——— two or more teachers as a team with rotation of team leader role.
   e. Our *sessions* are on ————————————— (day or days of week) from ——— to ——— (time).
   f. Our *curriculum material* is (series title or specific resource unit) ————————————— ; including teacher guidebook ——— , pupil book or leaflet ———, class packet ———, take home paper ———, other (identify) ———.

OBJECTIVE AND PURPOSES

2. The *objective of Christian education* is stated on page 10. Read this statement carefully for its significance to you as a teacher. Underline "agree" or "disagree" on the contiuum line below if you completely agree or disagree with this as the church's objective in Christian education. If you are somewhere between put a mark on the line to indicate how close or how far away from the two ends you feel you are.

agree ←———————————————→ disagree

If your mark is between the two ends, note below the changes you would make in the objective statement.	If you underlined *disagree* or were quite close to that end, write an objective statement as you think it should be.

3. My *purposes* in teaching are (four or more statements):

———————————————————————————————
———————————————————————————————
———————————————————————————————
———————————————————————————————

Other persons' statements of purpose may help you identify or clarify your own, whether yours are the same or different. The statements below are from two teaching teams in the same church in Missouri: They were written when both classes were using a unit called "Early Heroes of the Faith."

Teaching team, grades 3-4	Teaching team, grades 5-6
Our purposes in teaching are:	
that children will: • enjoy Sunday school • come to a commitment to God • see how the Bible relates to life • realize we are saved not by works but by God's grace	that children will: • grow in grace of God through relationship with others • learn to respect themselves and others, their rights and property, • grow in knowledge of teachings of Bible, to apply

• see how Old Testament relates to New Testament • learn difference between fellowship and salvation.	this knowledge to present day and their lives, • recognize human weaknesses in others, but mostly in themselves, • learn from early Bible heroes that we all make mistakes • learn that God loves, forgives, and accepts all his people even when they do wrong.
In further discussion the groups together looked at Christian education	
• as teaching content, concepts, values	• that children may know, be, and do as Christians.

If you wish, add other statements to your list of purposes:

_____

_____

ROLES AND RESPONSIBILITIES
OF TEACHERS (LEADERS) AND CHILDREN (LEARNERS)

4. Some of my thoughts on *learning* and *teaching* are:
   Learning is_____
   Teaching occurs when_____

   Effectiveness in the teaching-learning experience can be judged by_____.

5. *Functions* of leaders (teachers) and learners (children) are experienced differently from class to class. To the list below add other ideas that occur to you. Check (√) each function you feel is appropriate in a church school class of the age level you teach. Star (*) the eight to ten functions most used by you and by members of your class.

Functions in teaching-learning[1]				
(√) leader (teacher) (*)		(√) learner (child) (*)		
____ accepting child as person ____ answering child questions ____ asking child questions ____ challenging learner(s) ____ clarifying ideas ____ designing plans ____ directing learning process ____ enabling child in finding answers to questions ____ encouraging child initiative ____ establishing learning environment ____ evaluating progress toward goals ____ evaluating procedures ____ evoking human potential in each child ____ explaining information ____ facilitating learning ____ giving information			____ accepting other children as persons ____ accepting teacher as person ____ acquiring knowledge ____ asking questions ____ assisting other learners ____ choosing own activities ____ contributing ideas, information ____ creating and carrying out plans ____ determining own procedures ____ developing projects ____ discovering insights ____ doing work in pupil book ____ evaluating own behavior and participation ____ evaluating progress toward goal achievement ____ experimenting with materials	

____ guiding child in determining own procedures
____ guiding children in formulating own prayers
____ helping child achieve his or her own goals
____ helping child/group evaluate progress
____ identifying resources
____ instructing children
____ leading discussion
____ leading worship services
____ listening to child
____ praying
____ probing for feelings
____ probing for insights
____ providing learning resources
____ reading from Bible
____ remaining silent
____ responding to individual child
____ setting goals for the children
____ supporting child in skill development
____ stimulating child's desire to learn
____ structuring children's learning experiences
____ telling stories
____ witnessing to own Christian faith
____
____

____ exploring ideas
____ following teacher instructions
____ hearing Bible stories, verses, passages
____ inventing ideas
____ listening to other children
____ listening to teacher(s)
____ memorizing Bible verses
____ organizing ideas
____ participating in worship experiences
____ praying
____ reading Bible
____ reading for information
____ recalling information provided by teacher(s)
____ relating new insights to old ones
____ remembering information
____ researching for information
____ responding to God in spontaneous worship
____ searching for insights
____ seeking information
____ selecting own goals
____ studying the Bible
____ thinking for self
____ trying out new ideas
____ using familiar activities
____

Reread the functions for leaders and learners that you starred. What do these suggest about your teaching style? _____

6. *General responsibilities* of the teacher are carried out in different ways *in light* of a teacher's *self-expectations* and that teacher's perception of *expectations of others.* Read the statements in the blocks below. Add a statement of your own if none of these quite fits your ideas.

Identify the statement(s) most accurately expressing your perception of what is expected of teachers in your church, using

T for your view as a teacher or teaching team;
A for the expectations of the administrator or administrative committee that assigned you as teacher;
P for what the parents of your class members expect of you;
C for what the class members expect.

The four letters (T, A, P, C) may be in the same block or in two or more different blocks.

The teacher (or teaching team) should accept and carry out responsibility:
_____ for goal setting, preliminary planning, providing resources, room preparation, teaching procedures, evaluation of goal achievement.
_____ for goal setting, preliminary planning, collecting resources, room preparation; for guiding class (group) in development of plans or choosing among proposed procedures; for evaluation of goal achievement.

_____	for determining general direction of study, suggesting possible goals and alternative procedures; for guiding group in refining/defining own goals and plans, implementing their own goal-directed activities and evaluating achievement of group goals.
_____	for involving group members in the total teaching-learning process: goal setting, planning, determination of procedures and activities, securing resources, setting up learning situations (total group, small groups, individual assignments, learning centers), implementing plans, reaching conclusions, and evaluating both achievement of learning goals and effectiveness of group processes.
_____	for being sensitive to individual needs and interests; for developing teaching-learning plans (goals, resources, procedures, activities), taking into account interests of individuals in the group; for evaluating goals and plans in light of group progress and also individual responsiveness.
_____	for facilitating each learner's self-direction (individual decision-making and action) in selecting own goals, choosing independent activities for working toward goals; for providing or helping each learner to secure appropriate learning resources; for guiding learners in using freedom responsibly; for encouraging and enabling learners in self-evaluation of progress toward goals and of personal use of time and resources.

_____ for (your own statement)

These T, A, P, C expectations, as I see them,
(a) are all the same_____   (b) are all different_____
(c) have these two or three agreeing _____ , _____ , _____
These expectations, same or different affect my feelings or actions as a teacher in this way: _____

TEACHER QUALITIES AND SKILLS

(Each teacher brings to the learning situation his or her own personal qualities and teaching skills. Each likewise has limitations. Most teachers also are conscious of qualities or skills they would like to strengthen or develop.)

7. In column one below list *qualities* you possess that you feel are of value to you as a teacher. Star (*) two or more that you see as your greatest assets. In column two add to the partial list of qualities observed in other teachers. In the third column note qualities you wish to strengthen in yourself.

My own qualities	Qualities of others	Qualities I would like to develop
	• understanding of children of age-level taught • good basic biblical background • ability to communicate with others • sensitivity to persons • smiling countenance • knows what he or she believes theologically • openness to differing opinions	

• perceptive of causes of conflict • commitment to Christ • friendliness • expresses in daily relationships the reality of discipleship of Jesus Christ • •	

8. Use the next three columns to identify your own *skills*, skills observed in other teachers, your desired skills.

My personal skills	Skills of others	Skills I would like to develop
	• organizing ideas, plans • guiding children in art expression • bringing out children's ideas • telling stories • singing • playing piano • expressing ideas in art forms • listening to children •	

AFFIRMATIONS FOR TEACHERS

9. Below is a list of abbreviated affirmations, or guidelines. Add others that occur to you. On the left, check (√) each idea you consider important for teachers. On the right, star (*) affirmations you consciously reflect in your own teaching style.

Check (√)   Affirmations for Teachers   Star (*)

Children are
———   persons of individual worth   ———
———   responsive to God's love   ———
———   responsible in interpersonal relationships   ———
———   capable of making value-based decisions   ———
———   worthy of human dignity   ———
———

Learning in Christian education includes
———   biblical content, knowledge   ———
———   heritage of the faith community, the church   ———
———   meaning of the biblical message   ———
———   relationships with other persons   ———
———   theological concepts (God, man, natural world)   ———
———   significance of commitment to Jesus Christ   ———
———   values for living   ———
———   valuing processes (procedures for determining values)   ———
———

Learning in Christian education takes place
———   at crossing points of the gospel message and life experiences   ———
———   when a person is involved in discovery of the gospel message for his or her own life   ———
———   when the learner experiences meaning of God's love in her or his own life   ———
———

The teaching-learning experience is

——— designed for enabling the child to be aware of and respond to God's love ———
——— directed toward enabling each child to achieve his or her highest human potential ———
——— planned for facilitating the child's experience of discipleship to Jesus Christ and of being Christian in day-to-day living ———
——— personalized for each child ———
——— designed for involving children in learning through group relationships ———
——— ———

Teachers are

——— concerned for each child as a person ———
——— concerned for interrelationships of learners and of learners with leaders ———
——— confident in their own faith ———
——— facilitators of children's search for their own faith ———
——— open to persons of differing viewpoints on theology and education ———
——— sensitive to individual feelings, needs, interests ———
——— trusting of children as created by God with creative capabilities ———
——— witnesses to their own faith in word and deed ———
——— ———

DECISION-MAKING

Before you accepted the teaching assignment some decisions were made on behalf of your class by administrators—persons or committees—in your church, and by curriculum developers—committees, editors, writers. These decisions affect the teaching-learning experiences of your class. Many decisions are made by you as a teacher, by members of your class under your guidance, or by teacher(s) and children together.

10. The chart on page 55 lists some decisions made on behalf of or by learners in your class. For each idea on the left, check the person(s) or group(s) who makes decisions related to that idea.

If there are decisions in the chart that you feel should involve other decision-makers, in addition to or instead of the ones checked, note those decisions here and indicate who should be making them: __

_____

_____

Think about how you can facilitate this change (e.g., allowing children more freedom of choice, requesting changes by officials in your church, writing to the editor of your curriculum material).

SELF-IMPROVEMENT

(Each Christian's life is personal, unique.[2] So also is each teacher's (or team's) teaching style personal and unique. Each finds his or her own way of carrying out the assignment in the teaching ministry of the church *(didache)* under the continuing power and guidance of the Holy Spirit, the illuminating presence of God. Each determines how to offer children the proclamation of the gospel *(kerygma)* and, with the congregation, determines how to involve each child in the Christian community *(koinonia)* and in opportunities for service *(diakonia).* Through his or her teaching style, the teacher greatly influences the learning experiences of class members, and how these persons experience and express their own faith and life.)

To this point you have been involved in drawing your self-portrait through a reflection-assessment view of yourself as a teacher or member of a teaching team. You have identified skills and limitations, personal concerns in areas of child development, thoughts on what is to be taught and ideas of how teaching takes place. Now, you are ready for determining what changes, if any, you want to make and how you will try to do this.

11. The chart on page 56 is for sharpening your self-portrait. Use column one for listing your key characteristics and column two for noting your concerns to pursue and skills you wish to strengthen or develop. In column three check or add ways you can work on reshaping your teaching style.

DECISION MAKERS FOR MY CLASS

	Individual child	small group of class members	total group, class	the teacher	the teaching team	individual members of teaching team	pastor, education director	other church administrators	church committee, commission, board	parents	writers, editors, curriculum committee
make-up of class • number of children • age(s), grade(s) • number of teachers • number attending											
learning goals • possible goals • choice of goals											
curriculum materials • selection of curriculum resources • units (study areas) • suggested goals, content, procedures • use of unit suggestions											
planning • content to be explored, studied • general teaching-learning approach • in-class procedures											
learning activities • selection, choice • ways of developing, carrying out ideas • selection of out-of-class assignments • implementation of assignments											
evaluation • goal achievement • group process • individual involvement											

12. If you earlier described teachers you remember and noted ideas about yourself as teacher (page 41), compare your characteristics with the perceptions of yourself as you thought children see you. Do you see clues in your own profile (column 1, page 56) for reactions you attributed to children? How do your characteristics show similarities to those of your remembered teachers? Differences?

If you began your study with this chapter, you may wish now to use the charts on page 41. Or you may

Self-improvement

My key characteristics	Concerns to pursue; skills to strengthen	Ways of working on concerns, skills	(√)
		• trying a new idea from curriculum material • reading articles in teacher book • continuing other chapters in this book • participating in a skill workship • talking with someone about an idea I have • joining a Bible study group • taking enrichment or methods course • attending a laboratory school • studying a selected book from bibliography (page 95) • seeking ideas from children • participating in individual and group worship •	

wish to pursue some specific concerns from column two above (e.g., child development, chapter 4, or approaches in teaching-learning, chapter 9). You may prefer to use other self-directed or guided study indicated in column three above.

No two teachers are alike—but each of us has accepted the call to teach children. You, as a teacher, bring all that you are to the teaching-learning relationship with children and to the responsibility of service in the church's ministry through education.

Beatitudes for Teachers of Children
Blessed are you when your church says, "teach our children,"
   for then are you numbered among those who follow the great
   command, "Go, teach."
Blessed are you when children think of you as a trusted friend,
   for in establishing this relationship with the children you
   have attained one qualification of a good teacher.
Blessed are you when, with the children, you see beauty, love
truth, and live in righteousness,
   for as you teach you also will learn and grow.
Blessed are you when you are able to think of the needs of every
child as you plan your work,
   for understanding, affection, and security are essential to
   Christian life and growth.
Blessed are you when fathers and mothers recognize your sincerity of purpose,
   for Christian teaching is doubly sure when the home and church
   are in partnership.
Blessed are you when you are not satisfied with your ways of
teaching children,
   for self-improvement is always possible for those who earnestly
   desire to become better friends and guides of children.
Blessed are you when zeal for the kingdom of God fills your heart,
   for he who guides children in the way of love, good will, and
   righteousness is already building the kingdom of God.[3]

USING CURRICULUM MATERIALS AND OTHER RESOURCES

The child is not left to "just grow" like Topsy. Family, neighbors, community, school, church, TV, and other media join forces—or work in conflict—in providing a limited or wide range of learning opportunities. Each of these has a content—what is to be taught and learned—in relation to the objective of each.

Curriculum materials for the church school provide resources and guidance for developing teaching-learning plans that will enable persons to respond to God's love and to grow in Christian faith and commitment. (See objective, page 10.)

The scope of curriculum, as seen in most denominational and interdenominational curriculum resources, includes all of a person's relationships with God, with other persons, with nature, and with history. Principles and general organization for development of different study series will vary. Each series, or elective, is based on certain assumptions about persons and how they learn, what Christian education should include, and how teaching takes place.

Whatever curriculum material is provided for your class, you sift, expand, and in other ways adapt both content and procedures in relation to
• your own faith and commitment
• your purposes in teaching
• your perceptions of children and how they learn
• your own teaching style and current approach.

Even so, your church's choice of curriculum materials does affect your decision of what is to be taught and how—the curriculum of your class.

In *assessing curriculum resources,* what do you look for? In rating the ideas below, indicate what you feel your priorities really are at the present time (not what you think your priorities should be). Again, you can add other statements if you wish. This time you can give a cluster of three statements top priority, and three each for second and third rank.

I want materials I use to meet these criteria.		
Top Priority 1st____ 2nd____ 3rd____	Second 1st____ 2nd____ 3rd____	Third 1st____ 2nd____ 3rd____

1. They require little time for preparation.
2. They are supportive of the denomination in which I am a teacher.
3. I can understand them without having to struggle so hard.
4. They challenge me to grow.
5. They are similar to what I used as a child.
6. They provide handwork for students.
7. They are based on sound educational procedures.
8. They have a Bible story in almost every session.

9. The biblical concepts are appropriate for the age level.
10. The format is attractive.
11. I agree personally with the theology.
12. They allow for various personal interpretations.
13. They relate the biblical message to present-day life.
14. The children like them.
15.
16.

Which of the above statements did you give top rating? Which did you include in second and third place?

Now think of other persons in your church concerned with what is taught and learned in your class. Look at the priorities from their viewpoints. Which ideas do you think each of the following would choose as top priorities?

a. the children you teach   ____ ____ ____

b. the parents of those children   ____ ____ ____

c. other teachers in your church   ____ ____ ____

d. the majority of persons in your congregation   ____ ____ ____

e. the education commission or committee that selects the curriculm materials for your class

Are there differences of opinion between you and other teachers with whom you work (your team if you are on a teaching team, or other teachers in your church)? Or between teachers and any of the other groups above? [1]

Selection of curriculum materials is important: what materials are to be considered, who makes the selection, and how teachers influence the decision.

In your own church, who decides what curriculum materials are to be ordered for each class? Obviously the children do not make the choice, even though they are the ultimate users. Do they, through you, have any influence in the decision?

Turn to the chart on page 55. If you have already checked that chart, whom did you identify as making the selection of curriculum resources? If you made more than one check, star(*) the person or group having the most power in this decision. Now note any who influence the decision-making directly or indirectly.

Whoever makes the decision, you as a teacher have reason to be concerned about the choice. Presumably you were selected as a teacher because someone thought you had some

• knowledge and/or interest in the children—who they are and what they are to learn, and

• understanding of Christian education—what and how the children are to be taught in the church school. How can (or do) you and other teachers together make known your concerns on behalf of the children?

In some churches individual teachers or teaching teams are allowed to choose curriculum resources for the classes they teach. This enables teachers to take account of their own preferences—personal or on behalf of the children—for the one year or several years the children are with that teacher or team. A serious problem with this procedure is lack of continuity and development of the child's learning experiences as he or she moves from class to class.

It is important that consideration be given to what is available to the child from year to year as well as the specific resources to be used in any one year. For this reason, many churches have an education committee (or other official group) that chooses resources for all classes—children, youth, and adults. Teacher influence in selection of materials is through that committee.

You could request information on *principles* used by the committee in choosing materials, and then make suggestions for additional or alternate principles in light of your concerns as advocate for the children you teach. You might suggest that the committee—with interested teachers, parents, congregation members—explore the church school's responsibility for education in relation to the child's (person's) total Christian nurture and instruction in home and church. For this you might use chapter 3 of this book, "Christian Education in the Coming Years," (selected portions), or you might secure a resource on theological and educational foundations for curriculum in your own denomination.[2]

Another possibility is to look together at the *alternate curriculum resources* recommended by your own denomination. Many denominations have some kind of planbook or guidebook, or at least a statement, providing a basic description of various curriculum series and other materials recommended for churches of the denomination.

From time to time in other chapters of this book, materials are used from the current or an earlier *Planbook for Leaders of Children*. A major section of each Planbook is devoted to "Resources for Educational Ministry" for all teaching-learning settings: once-a-week study groups (Sunday school or other), vacation time groups, camping and other outdoor groups, and groups in informal settings. This annotated listing includes curriculum series and special electives.[3] Your denominational education headquarters or publishing house can provide available planbooks, guide sheets, and/or order blanks listing and describing recommended curriculum resources.

Recommendations of a given denomination may include that denomination's own publications (developed under an official curriculum committee), interdenominationally produced resources, and/or selected resources from other denominations.

FOR A TIME,   LEAP OF IMAGINATION!
LET'S TAKE A

Let's assume that you, as a local church representative, and I, as national education staff member, are participating in a meeting of our denomination's curriculum committee.

Editorial and program staff members have brought to the committee the problem of providing guidance and learning resources for teachers using a wide range of teaching-learning approaches. How can one curriculum series, or even several series, possibly be just what all these teachers want when their desires range from

(a) precise information to be taught _____ to
content resources for class selectivity,
(b) exact step-by-step teaching plans _____ to
guidance for creative development of local plans.

Offering more series from which to choose could better meet local needs—but local adaptation would still be necessary. The increased expense of producing this greater variety with more limited distribution would make purchase costs out of the reach of many churches.

The task of local church representatives on our imagined committee is to give guidance to denominational staff in developing resources. You are asked to think of three teachers you know (personality, ways of relating to learners, teaching approaches, theological views, educational background). Try to imagine yourself writing teacher guidance for these three teachers. Multiply these three by the hundreds of other teachers. Remember too that each of these teachers works with a number of children (few or many) with their differing learning needs, styles, and interests.

Now, your assignment with other committee members is to outline what you think these teachers have a right to expect of curriculum developers (national committee, editors, writers, publishers) in providing the materials teachers are to use.

_____
_____
_____
_____

Your ideas and those of other committee members help to guide policy for curriculum development, creation of series outlines, and each unit description for denominational or interdenominational production. This policy also guides decisions for recommendation of materials from other sources.

The meeting closes. You and I leave development of curriculum units in the hands of editors for working with writers and publishers in preparing new resources or making revisions, minor or major, in present resources for future use.

KEEP YOUR IMAGINATION ACTIVE!

You are aware that communication is two-way. You have been involved in sharing with national leaders some local church concerns. Now, out of your experience on the national committee you feel you have some thoughts you want to communicate with teachers in your own church. Taking the other side of "what teachers have a right to expect of curriculum developers," you decide to talk with teachers in your church (and perhaps in neighboring churches) about "what curriculum developers have a right to expect of teachers."

If you were working on these two ideas *for real*, what ideas in the following chart would you include? What would you add?

USING CURRICULUM MATERIALS AND OTHER RESOURCES

Teachers should be able to expect from curriculum developers	Curriculum developers should be able to expect of teachers
Sound theological base, rooted in biblical interpretation and guided by theological scholars.	Personal theological views, understandings, open to new insights from personal and group search for meaning.
Educationally and psychologically sound guidance in relation to children's readiness for learning.	Acquaintance with children in their own group, with awareness of varying capabilities and readiness for learning.
Age-level guidance based on understanding of life-span development, with focus on appropriate learning goals, content and procedures for the specific age-level.	Initiative in adapting goals, content, and procedures for meeting needs of children in the class—as individuals and as a group.
Dynamic writing that stimulates eagerness to pursue study and growth in discipleship to Jesus Christ.	Vital personal experience of commitment to Jesus Christ and desire to share that experience with others.
Trust of teachers in using the curriculum resources purposefully and creatively with their own children.	Trust of curriculum developers in taking account of local concerns and needs, as well as theological and educational know-how, in describing and producing resources for local church use.

Where did you come out in terms of reasonable expectations for teachers and curriculum developers? Look over your list above. What conclusions do you reach about development and use of curriculum resources. Some of my own conclusions are:

1. Any curriculum guidance developed by persons other than the users must be adapted, used selectively, and/or supplemented for most effective use by any group.
2. Local church educational and administrative decision-makers need
   (a) to explore with teachers views of goals, content, and procedures for Christian education, and
   (b) to examine various curriculum resources recommended in their denomination as bases for selection of materials to be provided for children and their teachers.
3. Teachers wanting step-by-step guidance need to examine whether they are willing to adapt teaching-learning plans to needs and interests of the children or are seeking an "easy" approach to teaching.
4. Any curriculum material can be adapted by leaders and learners for their own way of learning—teacher-directed, group-directed, self-directed—though some materials are more easily used with one or another of these three. (See chapters 5 and 6 on ways of teaching-learning)
5. A given curriculum series usually reflects one way of teaching primarily, with step-by-step procedures or more general guidance for teacher planning. Some series offer guidance for other ways of using the materials.
6. Teachers creating their own plans, using curriculum materials as resources and guides or using locally collected resources, need to examine their plans. Does their teaching-learning design enable children to use content and resources effectively in moving toward learning goals related to the general objective of Christian education?
7. Curriculum developers need to continue their efforts in providing curriculum guidance that is sound theologically, biblically, psychologically, educationally.
8. Curriculum developers need to provide support and guidance for teachers needing or wanting step-by-step guidance, and at the same time (in the same or a different curriculum series) to provide encouragement and guidance for teachers desiring freedom and ideas for varied approaches in learning and teaching.

Concerns of writers, editors, local church administrators, teachers in development and use of curriculum materials include

1. What learning goals does the writer have in mind for the children? How does the teacher (or teaching team) select from these, adapt them, or state other goals believed to be more appropriate for the class?
2. For what purposes are various activities suggested by writer(s)? Which purposes should the class pursue in relation to class goals? What activities proposed by the writer, ideas from the teacher(s), and suggestions from class members will be used?
3. How do curriculum planners, writers, and teachers each take account of learners' levels of capability and interests—not only in determining content and procedures, but also in anticipating extent of learner responsibility for his or her own learning?
4. How can writers help teachers achieve a balance of individual/independent and group/cooperative learning? What degree of balance is necessary? Desirable?
5. To what extent can or should writers be expected to provide
   • a teaching plan that can be followed step by step by a teacher or team, and/or
   • guidance enabling teachers to use curriculum resources in a variety of styles?
6. What basic teaching-learning style should writers and editors use in curriculum units? What variations from basic style (adaptations, combinations)? What guidance or clues (if any) for alternative approaches?
7. How can writers provide teacher guidance giving clear directions and also encourage/support/guide teachers in creative planning and teaching?

Earlier in this chapter we focused our attention more on curriculum development, but we have dealt with this in relation to local church use. Curriculum developers are continually reviewing, reinforcing, or revamping curriculum design and resources. (See chap. 3, notes 1 and 2, for references to current and recent studies.)

You can have a direct influence on your curriculum materials by writing or calling the editor of materials for your class. Be sure to include what you like about your present resources as well as your problems or concerns.

Let's turn our attention now to using curriculum materials in developing your own design for teaching-learning experiences with children. Use the guide on the following pages in connection with your present curriculum resources. Use all of the resources noted in the guide which are included in your teacher, pupil, and class pieces. If there are other materials in your curriculum resources, use those also. And don't overlook your central, primary curriculum resource—your Bible!

Using Curriculum Materials[4]

Examine your curriculum materials.
• one teacher or teaching team alone
• a teacher or teaching team with a counseling teacher or other educational supervisor or counselor
• in a workers conference of all teachers of children

Teacher Book—three major kinds of helps
• Suggestions and helps for teachers as they prepare
 —a meditation related to the current unit
 —Bible study guidance
 —description of the unit:
  what it is about
  ways children may learn and grow
  Bible resources
  other resources
• Session-by-session guidance:
 —focus or emphasis for the session
 —desired outcomes for children
 —activities for individuals and groups
 —resources to use: stories, songs, Bible references, audio-visuals, others
• Articles for all workers with children and for leaders of the specific age group
 —who the children are and how they learn
 —teacher planning
 —teacher growth and enrichment

Check below kinds of resources and types of help provided
• for teachers
• for children

The Bible—an essential resource
• for the teacher's own use
• for the teacher's use with children
• for individual and group use by older boys and girls
Teacher and student books indicate verses or longer passages for use in each study unit. Guidance for use of the Bible and specific biblical material is included in each teacher book.
Student Book—book or set of leaflets for each child
• Content—ideas for unit in
 —stories, songs
 —biblical material
 —thought stimulators
• Things to do
 —by individual child and by group
Story Paper—a take-home piece including
 —stories, things to do, other materials, related to class work
 —resources for leisure-time use
 —things to "do for myself" or with other family members

Class Packet—variety of resources for class
—pictures, art, or photography
—filmslips
—soundsheets or records
—games
—charts, murals
—songs
See teacher book for suggested use.

Additional Resources—books, audiovisuals
• preferred resources especially recommended for teachers or children in relation to the current unit
• other related resources for the church library, or for individual or class use

Consider what your church intends to happen through Christian education
• that children may be involved in situations where God's revelation may become personally meaningful to them
• that they may experience God's love and respond in faith and love. (See chapter 3, "Christian Education in the Coming Years.")

Explore ways the teacher or teachers of your class may plan for and with the children:
• teacher-directed
• group-directed
• self-directed
(See chapters 5 and 6.)

Develop general plans for the coming unit and specific plans for several sessions ahead. Use the current teacher book for your class for guidance in
• stating specific goals for the class and for individual children during this quarter (or other time such as a four-week unit or vacation school)
• selecting emphases for each session or for groups of sessions
• choosing activities through which children may explore concerns of the unit and may grow in relation to selected goals and emphases
• deciding when and how different resources will be used—student books, packet items, library resources—and how children will be guided in the use of these resources
• listing equipment and supplies needed throughout the unit, for several sessions, or for a single session
• deciding ways of evaluating the children's progress during the unit and at its close
(See chapter 9, "preparing for Teaching-Learning," and chapter 11, "Evaluating Teaching-Learning Effectiveness.")

Seek help in using curriculum materials in developing your own plans for learning experiences with children, from
• an educational leader in your own church
• an area children's worker or a leadership education instructor
• a public-school teacher
• someone to counsel with you or help you develop your teaching-learning approach.

Use your curriculum materials. Writers and editors prepare this guidance material for teachers who are using differing approaches. Each teacher or teaching team adapts goals and procedures for that teacher's or team's own class. (See chapter 10, "Exploring Alternative Approaches.")

Influence improvement in development of curriculum materials. Writers and editors experiment with ways of improving curriculum materials. They try to find ways of making the materials easier to use: content development, sentence length, type and size of print. They work on communication of concepts and possible teaching-learning procedures through the materials. Reactions from teachers help editors know which changes improve the usability of resources. Let your concerns be known by writing the editor of the materials you use. Include favorable reactions as well as suggestions for change.

Your own concepts of what is important *and* your *approach* in teaching-learning affect how you use your curriculum resources and the extent to which you use additional kinds of resources. What do you now consider as basic, essential curriculum material in addition to the Bible? What other resources do you use?

Check one of the following statements, or substitute your own.

_____ I use the student book or leaflet as basic; supplemented with ideas, resources from teacher book and class packet, possibly also from story paper.

_____ I use the curriculum package as a whole (teacher, pupil, class pieces) as basic, using selected resources from all of these; possibly using other resources suggested in teacher book (filmstrips, books, other).

_____ I use the curriculum package as basic; supplemented with other resources selected from teacher book recommendations and also other locally available resources.

_____ I use the _____ as basic; and I also use_____ .

How much freedom do you use in adapting writer suggestions for your own and your class's use? Do you sometimes use session ideas in a different order, or expand some sessions and condense or eliminate others? (See chapter 10 for different approaches for teaching and learning.)

Do you occasionally, frequently—or never—chop up and rearrange ideas and resources from your teacher and/or student materials (e.g., putting together ideas and instructions for dramatic activities from the entire unit for use by a drama interest group or for use in a learning center in which the drama content and procedure are appropriate)? How often do you use packet pictures or other items in more than one way—in ways suggested in teacher guidance and also in ways that occur to you as you plan for and work with your children?

Curriculum materials are tools. So are other resources. Keep your perspective on who you are teaching and why. (see chapter 4, "The Learner and Learning," and chapter 3, "Christian Education in the Coming Years.") Remember the objective of all church education is to enable persons to experience and respond to God's love and to be and become disciples of Christ. (See full statement of objective, page 10).

Utilize content from your curriculum materials and ideas for procedures as these have value for involving children in active learning experiences related to specific unit goals and to this overall objective.

Again, remember that the Bible is a primary resource and guide for you and your class. The gospel is taught and witnessed to through the lives and relationships of committed Christians and also through specific Bible study. (See pages 30-31 for more on children and Bible learning.) Your curriculum materials offer ways of involving children in discovering the meaning of the gospel for their lives and in exploring specific Bible passages.

In chapters 9 and 10 we shall explore ways teachers function and how children are involved in differing teaching-learning approaches.

PREPARING FOR TEACHING-LEARNING

A fifth-grade class caught the mood of the Bicentennial and turned a unit on church heritage and present reality into an exploration of local church history, culminating in a church-wide fair celebrating their local church heritage.

A group of first-graders visited a nursing home one Sunday morning. The class had spent a major part of the time for several previous sessions following the teacher's instructions for: discussing plans for the visit, making gifts to take, role-playing the visit, practicing favorite songs to sing, deciding rules for the trip. The Sunday following the visit, their conversation centered on how the people in the nursing home responded to the children and how the class members felt about the visit.

The family of a sixth-grader noticed a change in his Sunday morning behavior. He had always required several proddings to put aside the Sunday funnies when the rest of the family was ready to leave for Sunday School. Suddenly this boy became the one urging others, "Come on, its time to go." The parents, on visiting the older-elementary class, saw the boy bound into his room, choose his area for research, and go to work using resources and guides provided in the area. A look around the room showed several learning areas related to the study theme "How We Got Our Bible." This boy had chosen the archaeological area.

In all three of the above situations, children became involved in learning experiences under the guidance of church-school teachers. In each case, teacher(s) and children used ideas and resources from regular curriculum units and pertinent biblical passages. Each class made some adaptation or change in suggested procedures. Yet each was different in its primary way of learning (group-directed, teacher-directed, self-directed) and in general approach (group process, teacher-planned project, learning centers).[1]

Let's look more closely at these three situations.

Group I: Fifth-grade class with one teacher—Local church festival

Teacher and class began with plans outlined in teacher's guide-book, studying heritage and present reality of the church.

Group members saw parallel of church heritage study to current Bicentennial emphasis and suggested class focus on exploring local church history.

Teacher responded, moved with group into group process of determining what they wanted to find out, how they would proceed, what they would do with their findings.

The way of teaching-learning changed from teacher-directed study to *group-directed* project development.

The approach of the class after deciding on the project was *group process* in goal-setting, procedure determination, committee and individual assignments, process of developing research findings into exhibits for the church festival, enlisting women of the church in providing refreshments, bringing the congregation into the festival celebration of the congregation's heritage.

The subject of church heritage and present reality was dealt with in relation to local history and life. The goal—a sense of belonging to and working in The United Methodist Church came alive for the boys and girls.

Group 2: First-graders with three teachers—Nursing home visit

Teachers adapted plans from a curriculum unit on "We Are the Church" for guiding children toward realization that the church is being the church when it is worshiping, in showing concern for persons who are ill, in teaching and learning, and through working together.

The visit to the nursing home was a teacher-directed project including several related activities involving the children.

The visit was both tradition and new experience: tradition for teachers and persons at the home, new for this year's first-graders.

The children's involvement was primarily in following teacher instructions, with some creativity in development of teacher-planned gifts and in naming some rules for the trip.

Learning was evidenced in the post-visit conversation indicating that a few, if not all, of the children had gained some insight into the feelings of the people in the home and had achieved some understanding of being the church in service to others and in working together.

While the general plan for learning in this class was primarily teacher-directed, there was evidence of Christian concern for persons among teachers and children and of child learning through relationships.

Group 3: Older elementary class—Learning Center

Teaching team of several teachers from the fifth and sixth grades used content and activities from the entire unit in designing learning areas and in developing guides for individual use by boys and girls of the combined fifth and sixth grade class.

Each learning area included three kinds of activities:
• one or more calling for use of student book,
• one or more requiring use of the Bible,
• one or more offering ways for individuals to express ideas, thoughts, feelings, findings.

In each area teachers provided a variety of resources: Bibles, books, pictures, filmstrips, objects, packets of materials, art supplies.

Each child used his or her own student book as it was needed. Each girl or boy selected an area for research, continuing in the same area or moving to another each succeeding Sunday. Some activities were starred for use by each participant in an area. Other activities were optional. Each person set her or his own work pace and order of activities. Each person had a large envelope for keeping a personal record of areas and activities used and for storing work sheets, art work, Bible references, other materials of his or her own choosing.

Teachers served as providers of resources and facilitators of *individual learning procedures.* For some children needing extra help with *self-direction* or with procedures for specific activities, teachers served as supporters, interpreters, or guides. For children wanting an adult with whom to share or discuss a developing idea or someone to provide additional information, teachers served as listeners, conversationalists, reactors, resource persons.

From time to time different children were observed serving as facilitators or resource persons for other learners, or were seen using resources together, doing research in a small group, sharing ideas. In an occasional sharing time for the total class, further exchange of findings and individual ideas took place.

Learning was reflected in discoveries reported by many of the children on a given Sunday or in group sharing times, and in individual writings or art expressing thoughts and feelings.

Change of attitude toward Sunday school attendance and Bible study was observed in the boy in the illustration and in many other children.

We have identified the above teaching-learning experiences as group-directed, teacher-directed, or self-directed in relation to who made major decisions. We noted, however, that both teacher(s) and children made some decisions. Teachers, in each case, made some plans, decisions, and preparations. The distinctiveness of the particular way of learning is seen in the kinds of decisions made by individual children, the group, or the teacher(s) and in the extent of child decision-making and self-direction.

In the above illustrations, we observe other differences:
• a single teacher or a teaching team;
• class procedure: group process, project, learning center areas. (See chapter 10 for more on alternative approaches.)
• specific methods or activities (research, exhibit preparation, church festival, gift-making, nursing home visit, expressing ideas, discussing feelings);
• teacher (teaching team) relationship to children as individuals and group: director of learning activities, group member with boys and girls in planning and action, facilitator.

Let's move from these three illustrations to our own classes. Have these situations reminded you of specific teaching-learning experiences of your class? Or have you thought of other methods or general approach you use with your class?

In chapter 5 we give two broad classifications of ways of teaching: teaching alone and teaching on a team. While I find myself at present in one of these two categories, *who I am as a teacher* is more specific. Who you are as a teacher is more specific and more personal. The child's way of learning is greatly affected by the teacher's way of functioning in the teaching-learning group.

Check below the description that best identifies you now as teacher. Star the identification you would prefer (same or different).

	present (√)	preferred (*)
I see myself as a single teacher,		
• viewing teacher as one who knows or has access to knowledge and viewing child as one to be taught.	_____	_____
• viewing children and myself as learners, and myself as also teacher.	_____	_____
• viewing myself and the children as both learners and teachers, with myself as having additional teacher responsibility.	_____	_____
• viewing_____	_____	_____
I see myself as member of a teaching team,		
• functioning as a leader with assistants or helpers in the style of the teacher who		

knows and whose helpers serve to help extend teacher coverage to children being
taught.   _____   _____
• functioning as a co-leader in planning and a co-learner with the children in carrying
out plans.   _____   _____
• functioning as a co-leader in planning, and as a group member with children in
completing and carrying out plans and in evaluation.   _____   _____
• functioning as_____
_____   _____   _____

In chapters 5 and 6 we observe that one teacher teaching alone or a teaching team can
• determine the extent to which learners are allowed or encouraged to make decisions in specific areas of
choice;
• design the teaching-learning plan for one of the three ways of learning (self-directed, group-directed,
teacher-directed), a modification of one of these ways, or a combination of two or three ways, according to
teacher preference or anticipated learner needs for leader input and process direction; building group
relationships; or choice or pacing of individual learning:
• direct / guide / assist learners in securing information, discovering meanings, developing values;
• be creative in preliminary planning, in directing / guiding children in learning procedures, in evaluating
goal achievement.

We have already observed some distinctions in teaching alone and teaching with a teaching team (chapter 5).
We now recall such distinctions and add several observed tendencies of a single teacher or a team.

Single Teacher	Teaching Team
Has full responsibility for • making all leader preparation • deciding how she or he will work with children • relating to individual learners and to the group • providing resources for learning.	Has shared responsibility for • preparation • leadership role each will have in working with children • relationships with individual learners and with the group • provision of resources for learning.
Can do teacher planning at own convenience, or seek help from counseling teacher or other supervisor or friend.	Shares in cooperative planning at time set by lead teacher or team; may seek help from counseling teacher, supervisor.
Is dependent on his or her own teaching skills or capabilities, or solicits help from persons with special skills (class members, friends, others).	Capitalizes on varied skills of team members; teaches one another needed skills; solicits special help (from class members, friends, others).
Is alone responsible for collecting and organizing resources, preparing learning environment (room arrangement, way of making resources available, use of charts, pictures, etc.).	Shares responsibility for collecting and organizing resources, preparing learning environment (room arrangement, way of making resources available, use of charts, pictures, etc.).
Has a tendency to provide for teacher-directed learning, with teacher • determining goals and approach • expecting all class members to do same activities at the same time, possibly allowing some choice in limited areas (e.g., writing or drawing) • serving as director of learning (content and procedures).	Is more likely than a single teacher to do group teaching, with • teaching team making broad, general plans; • children and teachers sharing in determining specific goals and plans; • a team member serving as process director and team providing needed resources.

May involve children in a group process in which boys and girls with the teacher make major decisions and all work together as learners.	May, as a team, provide for teacher-directed learning, with • one teacher serving as learning director for teachers and children, or • members of team fulfilling predetermined assignments for direction of learning.
May prepare for and facilitate a selected approach to self-directed learning. May_____ _____	May together prepare for and facilitate an approach to self-directed learning. May_____ _____

As a single teacher or as a teaching team, my (our) ways of functioning in planning and working with my (our) class can best be described as follows:

In the three illustrations at the beginning of this chapter, we identified a few activities: research, preparing exhibits, holding a festival, expressing ideas or feelings in some art form, making gifts, role playing, singing, visiting, studying the Bible, using student book.

In the following chart check (√) activities used by your present class, or by similar groups of the same age(s). Star (*) ten to twenty or twenty-five activities your class currently uses most frequently. Put a question mark (?) by methods not now used, or infrequently used, that you think you might be able to use appropriately with your present class. Add other activities that occur to you, checking, starring, or questioning these also.[2]

Activities	√	*	?	Activities	√	*	?
• acquiring information • asking questions (who, why, what, how, what for?) • asking riddles • acquiring Bible skills • building with blocks • bringing pet to class and letting others enjoy it • building Palestinian house • building with wood • climbing • caring for a class pet • collecting objects • creating music • creating scenery for play • checking multiple-choice answers • developing exhibits • developing choral reading • determining goals • discovering living things outdoors • discussing personal (group) concerns, problems				• discussing meaning of a biblical passage • discussing principles, values • discussing what happened in a story and why • doing friendly acts • doing rhythmic movement to music • dramatizing a story • drawing pictures • eating a snack • enjoying companionship of another person (group) • enjoying nature objects • entertaining guests • expressing feelings (in movement, art, etc.) • expressing ideas in art forms (writing, drawing, painting, music, etc.) • expressing ideas or feelings verbally • examining nature objects • finding answers for puzzles through reading in Bible or student book • finding information through research			

Activities	√	*	?	Activities	√	*	?
• going on a trip (another church, synagogue, community center, elsewhere)				• operating filmstrip projector or other visual equipment			
• hearing stories				• operating record player			
• hearing teacher express own assurance of God's love				• picking up and putting away toys, work materials			
• hearing teacher pray				• painting pictures (single picture, frieze, mural, etc.)			
• having a "picnic" in room or outdoors				• participating in conversation or discussion			
• helping another child (to read, make something, climb, etc.)				• planning and doing a service project			
• holding Bible while a teacher reads from it				• planning and participating in worship			
• home-living play (dolls, house-keeping, dressing-up, meal preparation, etc.)				• planning and preparing exhibits			
				• playing games			
• identifying objects by feel (size or shape) or by sound				• playing piano, autoharp, other instruments			
• imagining being in another place or situation				• playing roles, being someone else, pretending			
• imagining endings for incomplete stories				• playing with moving toys (cars, doll buggies, etc.)			
• initiating a conversation				• playing with other children			
• inquiring for information				• praying			
• interviewing (minister, church member, another child)				• putting puzzle pieces in place			
• introducing a visitor				• quizzing classmates			
• learning new songs				• reading Bible passages			
• learning to find Bible passages				• reading books			
• listening for outdoor sounds				• reading in student book			
• listening to biblical stories and other passages				• receiving a visitor (minister, a baby, etc.)			
• listening to instructions				• responding to teacher's greeting			
• listening to music				• recalling Bible stories, verses			
• looking at pictures and picture books				• requesting information			
				• requesting interpretation			
• making gifts (book marks, decorated flowerpots, etc.)				• role playing situations			
• making greeting cards				• rolling ball to another person			
• making plans for group activity				• seeing a rainbow			
• making rules				• seeing teacher use Bible			
• making up a story				• sharing a toy			
• making posters, displays				• sharing work materials			
• memorizing Bible passages				• singing a song			
• molding clay figures, objects				• sleeping			
				• smelling foods, flowers, other odors			
• naming items in a picture				• taking off and putting on wraps			
• naming objects (in room, on a walk, in a closed box, etc.)				• talking about pictures			
				• tasting different foods			
• observing animals				• telling familiar stories			
				• using Bible passage or song as a choral reading			
				• using big-muscle equipment (slide, walking board, etc.)			

Activities	√	*	?	Activities	√	*	?
• using construction materials—cardboard, wood • using reference books to find information • using student book, leaflet • viewing filmstrip, slides, film—alone, with others • visiting another class				• visiting minister, another church leader • visiting shut-ins • watching filmstrip or slides with whole class • watching a bird or animal • watching raindrops • working on a committee • writing (or dictating to teacher) original stories, songs, prayers			

Look back over your starred activities. To what extent are these most used activities of similar types, or different?

_____

_____

Are both mental and physical action included? Yes ____ , No ____ . Are the activities primarily self-directed ____ , teacher-directed, ____ , or group-directed ____ ?

As indicated earlier, this chart includes activities frequently used by church-school groups. Selection for a particular group relates to the age or grade range of the class and to capabilities and interests of individual children. The objective of education and the teacher's (team's) purposes in teaching further influence choice of activities.

Many activities are suitable for children of a given age and appropriate for church use, but not all activities are equally desirable at a given time. Goals for the current study unit and your purpose in using a particular activity help in sharpening how the activity is to be used. In a unit on worship, older elementary boys and girls might write a prayer as one way of worshiping God. In a unit on God's world, kindergarten children might dictate to a teacher some ideas to be included in a thank-you prayer. Purposes in using particular songs at different times might include: exploring ideas to which the song could contribute, expressing feelings, singing praise to God, having fun with rhythm or word sounds, playing a singing game.

Bible stories and other passages may be read or heard for information related to the current study, for exploring meanings in the situation, for discovering the message for living today. Bible passages may be read in study, in worship, as stories or verses in conversation time, depending on the reason for using the particular passage in a particular session. Further, Bible passages might be dramatized, used as choral readings, sung, memorized. So too are there many reasons and ways for using other resources and activities.

In this chapter we have given attention to the relation of teacher or teaching team to the children. We have looked also at some of the many activities from which teachers choose in planning for teaching-learning with their classes. Early in the chapter we saw how three classes used different learning approaches (overall plans for teaching-learning): group process, teacher-directed project, learning-center approach.

In chapter 10 we will explore a number of different *approaches in church education.* Each approach makes use of many of the activities listed on the preceding pages.

EXPLORING ALTERNATIVE APPROACHES

Teaching-learning unit, individualized instruction, team teaching, learning center—you name it! There are many different ways of organizing goals, resources, and activities into a plan for involving class members in the teaching-learning experience.

In this chapter we identify and examine a number of *approaches in church education,* noting variations of some:
- a session-at-a-time approach, teacher presentation or child activity form,
- a unit approach, single teacher or teaching team,
- group teaching and other group process approaches,
- intergenerational approach,
- individualized learning, independent study,
- learning center approach, including open classroom and other forms.

We might think of the teaching-learning approach as a covering canopy for holding together all parts of the learning experience—the way teachers and learners work toward learning goals using selected resources and procedures.

Review the illustrations at the beginning of chapter 9, noting the three different approaches: group process initiated by the class, teacher-directed project, learning center.

Now think of your own class and your current approach in working with the children. Describe briefly your present approach by completing the following three sentences.

In planning for teaching-learning, my major focus is on

(check one or write your own major focus):

(a) the things I will do in guiding the class session. _____
(b) the content to be studied/taught. _____
(c) the goals of the unit/session and activities for achieving those goals. _____
(d) procedures for involving the child in exploring content and working toward goals. _____
(e) _____

During the class session the teacher (team) responsibilities are:_____
_____
_____
_____

The children are involved in learning through:_____
_____
_____

As we explore the different approaches, we will be increasingly aware that it is impossible to isolate one approach entirely from any other. For instance, individualized learning is often associated with the learning-center approach, but individualization can be used in some ways in group teaching or in a unit approach. The intergenerational approach might take the form of any of the other approaches, but it has some of its own unique features that should be noted.

The church education approaches included on the following pages are those which most often come to my attention as I work with teachers and other leaders across the church. There are other approaches and other variations or combinations of these approaches.

The validity of each approach is in its potential for enabling the child to grow
- in and toward faith in God, commitment to Jesus Christ, response to God through Christ, empowered by the Holy Spirit; and
- in being and becoming Christian in all relationships.

As we look at each approach, we will note one or more identifying features. We will highlight the focus of the teacher's or team's planning and preparation, and will add additional comments as needed for interpretation of the approach. Naturally, within one chapter it is not feasible to give a thorough interpretation. Resources on some of the less familiar approaches are included in the Bibliography.

How teachers use curriculum materials in teaching-learning with children is considered in chapter 8. Evaluation as an essential part of the total teaching-learning process will be reviewed in chapter 11.

SESSION-AT-A-TIME APPROACH

- Teacher preparation is one week (or day) at a time.
- Continuity in content and procedure from one session to another is primarily in recall from previous session(s). There is little, if any, looking ahead.

• This approach is usually used by a single teacher with from three or four to fifteen or twenty children. Rarely is this approach used by a teaching team.

1. Session-at-a-time, teacher presentation form.

Focus in planning is on *content* to be covered and how the teacher will present the "lesson." Teacher frequently uses only that part of the session material in the child's book or leaflet which is informational. Sometimes the teacher adds further information from the teacher book.

The teacher's plan identifies activities mainly in terms of what the teacher is to do: tell or read a story, read a Bible passage, show and talk about a picture, present certain facts, pray on behalf of the children.

The children's activity is primarily listening. They may sing a song or two. Further child involvement, if any, is usually of the content feedback type: memorizing and repeating Bible verses, answering questions. In using pupil book or leaflet, children follow teacher instructions in using pages that provide information or call for filling in information type answers.

Other resources used are generally pictures from the class packet, sometimes a filmslip from the same packet. Some teachers use an additional storybook for more information.

In some classes early comers are allowed to play, look at or read books, work puzzles. Children and teacher see these activities as preliminary to the lesson. The class begins for them when the teacher uses an "opening prayer" or begins giving information or instructions.

If this approach is used by a teaching team, teacher responsibilities are divided in terms of what part of the presentation each will do, or assignments each will take (teach, play the piano, serve as secretary).

Whether or not the lesson for the day is covered, the teacher moves on in the next session to content ideas for that day.

The lecture as a means of teacher input is often used with youth and adults but very rarely with children. In some classes, however, teacher input using stories, Bible materials, and informational data is closely akin to a lecture.

Child application of learning is an out-of-class child responsibility.

A frequent concern of teachers is that the curriculum materials do not provide enough story and information type resources for teacher input for the entire session.

2. Session-at-a-time, child activity form.

This approach is used most often by a single teacher. When a team uses it, the teachers generally plan in terms of what activities will be used in a given session and each teacher's responsibility in that session ("I'll tell the story, you show the children how to make Bible bookmarks, and he will guide the action song.") Teacher responsibility is seen primarily as teacher input and process instruction.

The *focus* of teacher planning is on *both content* to be presented by teacher or provided through pupil book or leaflet and other resources (pictures, visuals); and *activities* that will interest the children and give them something to do related to the session goal and content (e.g., making a gift for the minister in unit on church workers, or drawing Palestinian house when learning about Jesus' boyhood).

This approach is usually teacher-directed in that the teacher makes all major decisions—what is to be learned and how—and directs all or most child activities step by step. Often this is more nearly a teacher presentation with child feedback, but sometimes story and Bible material are used for stimulating the children's thought and expression of ideas in conversation and art.

The teacher selects activities for each session in terms of child interest and the possible contribution of each activity to the achievement of session goals.

Occasionally, a teacher using a session-at-a-time approach will allow children some freedom of choice:
• in art activities (using cut-out pictures or making their own drawings),
• in interest activities (drama or art) for individuals or small groups,
• in selection of a total class activity.

Incomplete activities may be continued in the next session but seldom are. Sometimes a child is encouraged to finish individual work at home. The same or similar activity may be used in a later session, but seldom is an activity planned for continuing use in two or more sessions (e.g., different stories may be dramatized on successive Sundays, but seldom is a drama planned and developed over several sessions).

A concern of some teachers using this approach is that curriculum materials have more in a session (content and activities) than they can use in the limited time available. When teachers focus on content emphasis and activity selection in relation to goals for their own class, choosing from among the suggested activities becomes easier and there is less concern about covering the lesson in terms of equal use of each page of teacher and pupil book material. In fact, many teachers welcome a variety of activities and ideas on ways of using resources, so that they can choose ways of involving their children according to the boys' and girls' own interests and capabilities.

UNIT APPROACH

- Teacher preparation is for an entire unit or subunit (series of sessions) with guided learning experiences related to a single theme or unit title.
- Continuity in content and procedures from session to session is a part of the teacher plan.
- This approach is increasingly used by those teaching alone, but is more often used by a teaching team.
- A unit approach may be either teacher-directed or group-directed. Unit goals and activities may be adapted for self-directed learning.

3. Single-teacher unit approach.

Focus in teacher preparation is on *unit purposes* as these relate to overall learning needs of children in the class, and on *child activities* that will enable children to achieve unit purposes. Session purposes and activities are adapted in relation to the longer term plan. Basic content is developed through procedures designed for several successive sessions (or entire unit) rather than for separate single sessions.

Unit planning includes consideration of
- unit theme and purpose as stated in the curriculum materials, and as restated or affirmed by the teacher;
- concerns of boys and girls related to the unit focus;
- selection of biblical material, stories, songs, other resources in light of both the children's concerns and teacher's purposes;
- choice of activities appropriate to the children, to the unit content, and to the available time and resources.

Activities in the first session (or early sessions) are planned for involving boys and girls in initiating the unit content and plans for succeeding sessions. Throughout the unit the children participate in a variety of total-class and small-group or individual activities for exploration, study, and sharing of ideas and feelings.

Some content ideas and some activities are completed in a single session; others continue for several sessions or throughout a unit.

The teacher determines the extent to which children are involved in decision-making. Children's planning may be limited to individual selection of an interest group for a portion of class work, or to a total group choice between two similar activities. On the other hand, children may be involved with the teacher in early sessions of the unit in setting their own specific goals and in selecting activities and materials for working toward those goals.

One concern of a teacher alone in unit teaching is how he or she can guide children in several simultaneous groups. Another concern is how to help an absentee get on board with the group when he or she returns to class. Many teachers find that the children can be quite helpful in these situations. If plans and procedures are clear, older boys and girls can work in committees with a group chairperson. The teacher or another child can help one who has been absent to know what the class or small group is working on and what the goals are.

4. Team-teaching unit approach.

The *focus* is both on unit *purposes* and *child learning* and on *how teachers will work together*.

Team teaching, as used in church education, is an approach *characterized by* the *way two or more teachers work together*. Variations in this approach result from differing perceptions of what being a teaching team means:
- a lead teacher with helpers or assisting teachers;
- a cooperative team relationship with shared responsibility, with lead teacher as coordinator of planning;
- a team of teachers planning together then serving as "the teacher" in a teacher-directed relationship with the children;
- a cooperative team relationship both in planning and in working with the children, teachers leading together rather than taking turns as teacher;

• teachers as team in planning; children and teachers all working together in class in developing and carrying out plans (see group teaching, approach #5).

Some of the advantages in team teaching are:

• sharing of responsibility in planning and in working with children.
• division of tasks for collecting resources, arranging room, preparing for various activities;
• supportiveness of one another as leaders;
• availability of a teacher to an individual child with a special need, or to a small group requiring guidance;
• supplementing of one another's teaching skills, and learning from one another;
• increased participation of a group of teachers and children working together rather than a teacher with a group of children;
• continuity of the teacher relationship with children when one teacher is absent.

Two or more teachers may be assigned to a class. They become a team and develop their own team style as they plan, pray, study, and teach together. Teachers might strengthen their "teamness" by sharing personal concerns and by exploring together their anticipations and uncertainties in being team members. They can help one another grow as teachers through affirming each one's teaching strengths and by helping one another develop new insights and skills.

Team members sometimes have difficulty knowing when to take the initiative in making on-the-spot decisions lest other teachers be disconcerted. Some teams develop ways of clearing signals with one another within, as well as between, sessions. Others involve the boys and girls in determining any change of direction during a session and in projecting plans for later sessions.

Evaluation in team teaching includes exploring ways of improving working relationships between or among teachers as well as effectiveness of goal achievement and class procedures of the learning group.

GROUP PROCESS APPROACH

• A single teacher or group of teachers works with class members in determining group goals, plans, and procedures; and in evaluating progress toward goals.
• The primary way of learning is group directed, with children and teachers together making major decisions.
• Preliminary planning by teachers includes listing possible goals and activities and determining procedures for enabling children and teachers together to set class goals and develop plans for working toward those goals.
• In class sessions teachers give special attention to guiding group process.

5. Group teaching.

The *focus* in group teaching is on *involvement* of group members *in the total process* of goal-setting, planning, implementation of plans, and evaluation. Occasionally a single teacher uses group teaching with a class, but more often this approach is used by a teaching team.

The distinctiveness of this approach in church education is that the *group* includes both *children and teachers*. The concept of "all learners and all teachers" is integral in this way of combining group process and team teaching.

Major class decisions are made by the group. The degree of *child involvement in decision-making* is related to maturity of the children in skills of choosing and of assuming responsibility for their choices. This maturity is both a matter of developmental level (see chapter 4) and an outgrowth of previous experience in making choices and acting on those choices. With any group at any age or grade level, group teaching includes both individual valuing, choices, actions, and interrelationships of group members in group decision and action.

Before young children are ready for group planning the teaching team plans opportunities for each child to choose activities he or she will do. Teachers listen to children's questions and expressions of interest as bases for making plans. Ideas that originate with the children are incorporated into the plans. As individual children are involved in small group or total group activities, the children have experience according to their capabilities in being responsible members of the group.

Older boys and girls are able to assume even more direct responsibility for helping to determine the purposes of a unit, the questions for which they want to find answers, the service they want to perform, and how to work so that their objectives will be achieved. They are able to evaluate their progress in terms of "how are we doing?" They can summarize at the close of a unit: what have we learned? how have we grown? what new skills have we mastered? Social development—the ability to live and work helpfully with others—is an important part of Christian growth. It comes only through experiences in responsible participation in group life and work.[1]

In church education, group teaching is one approach incorporating this aspect of Christian living in the total teaching-learning experience.

Some of the advantages in group teaching are
• learning through living and working together as a group,
• experiences in exploring alternatives as bases for making group decisions,
• give and take in group process of making choices and in taking responsibility for individual and group implementation of plans,
• more opportunity than in some other approaches for boys and girls and teachers to know one another as persons through working and worshiping together,
• involvement in, rather than simply talking about, being responsible group members.

Teachers, out of their more extensive experience, knowledge, and preparation, fulfill special group member responsibilities in providing guidance, information, and resources. Teachers have a unique opportunity in group teaching to portray the church as the people of God and a supportive fellowship of Christians in interrelationships among teachers and with children.

Some teachers feel ill at ease in situations permitting girls and boys to make decisions, especially if the children are to be full participants in the total group process. For these teachers a beginning step toward group teaching might be to risk allowing class members limited choice within a more teacher-directed learning situation. Or a teacher inexperienced in group process might observe a class using group teaching and join in evaluation with the teaching team.

6. Group problem solving.

The *focus* of this form of group process is on *skill development* in goal determination, participation and leadership, the process of decision-making, dealing with conflict, group cohesion, problem solving, interpersonal effectiveness.

The *distinctive feature* in this approach to teaching-learning is the utilization of *group dynamics* for enabling group exploration and solution of a group problem or concern. Roles of group members relate to both group maintenance functions and task-oriented functions. The role of the leader(s) is primarily as expediter or guide.

Techniques of problem-solving are used in group teaching (#5 above). Group problem-solving procedures are at times used in other teaching-learning approaches in relation to particular problems that arise.

As a learning procedure in the church school, group problem-solving is more likely to be used by youth or adults. This approach is more typical in self-determining groups with elected leaders than in classes with assigned teachers. Group problem solving as the general overarching approach is seldom used with children. An exception is special groups such as a volunteer neighborhood group or other short time or consecutive day group.

INTERGENERATIONAL APPROACH

• Any intergenerational learning experience assumes that children, youth, and adults—all together or in some combination across generations—can learn together.
• Younger and older persons alike contribute to one another's learning experience.
• A committee, teacher, or teaching team might be responsible for developing preliminary plans.
• The nature of the experience might be a study-activity class, a fellowship event or series of occasions, a worship service with active group member involvement, or any of a number of other inter-age opportunities.
• Intergenerational settings for education provide planned opportunities for nurture, discussion, and training in which a major purpose is interaction and mutual ministry among persons of two or more generations.[2]
• The church is intergenerational in its inclusion of persons of all generations (children, youth, young adults, adults, older adults). Intentional intergenerational groups involve all group members in enabling one another to be Christian, to know their heritage and faith as Christians, to do (live and act) as Christians.[2]

7. Intergenerational class.

The *focus* is on persons of *different generations learning from* and *with one another.* In the intergenerational class, the teaching team or planning committee might be all adult or it might include representatives of different age levels.

The class may be primarily teacher- or committee-directed, or group members may be involved in group planning and action. In either case, planning goals, teaching-learning methods, and specific activities take account of needs, interests, and learning potential of all persons of all ages included in the group. An intergenerational experience must have face-to-face interaction among persons of two or more generations.

A part of the design of anyone conducting an intergenerational group is for children and older persons alike to accept themselves and others as persons, each with his or her own learning potential and capabilities for contributing to the learning of others.

The uniqueness of the intergenerational approach is in the ways persons of different generations relate to one another in the teaching-learning experience. Content is chosen with all participants in mind. Procedures take account of the ways persons of various maturity levels can learn as individuals and in interaction with persons of other generations.

One of the big concerns of persons preparing for this approach is whether adults can learn as adults while being involved with children, or with children and youth, who likewise are learning at their own level. There is a temptation for adult group members to move into teacher roles, supervising the children rather than working with them on mutual interests and concerns.

This approach has high potential for experiential learning for persons of wide age span (children-youth-adult) or of divided generations (children-adult) in a covenant community of persons striving to grow in Christian faith and life. The effective intergenerational class involves each person not only at his or her own maturity level but also in interaction with persons of the same and different generations.

INDIVIDUALIZATION

- Persons, with their individual interests and capabilities, are central in teacher planning.
- Individualization may include one or more of the following:
  - self-pacing for some or all students,
  - provision of resources selected for individual children,
  - freedom of choice in ways of working toward common goals,
  - provision of learning guides including options for individual decision-making,
  - special guidance and support for children with particular learning difficulties,
  - the child's determination, with teacher counsel, of his or her own goals and ways of working toward those goals.

8. Individualized learning approach.

The *focus* in planning is *on individual* children and how they might participate in the learning experience with satisfaction and a sense of achievement.

Individualized learning in church education is most often used by a teaching team using some form of learning-center approach (see #10 and #11). In these situations, learning is primarily self-directed with the teacher(s) providing resources and alternative ways of working toward goals.

Teachers may use some individualization within a unit approach (#3 or #4) or in group teaching (#5), with provision for choice of individual and/or group activities. At times the child is allowed freedom in developing an idea or in doing a piece of work in his or her own way as a contribution to the total group teaching-learning experience. Occasionally, teachers provide resources and special guidance for children with particular learning difficulties. (See pages 45-46 for identification of some special learning needs.)

Individualization as an approach calls for organization of *resources* and development of *guides for* enabling each *child to function in a self-directed way* according to his or her capabilities.

This approach may be used by a single teacher but is most often used by a teaching team. Team members together determine:
- scope of content (usually using a curriculum unit for basic resources),

• extent and type of individualization to be used and extent of individual self-direction and responsibility anticipated for each child,
• boundaries of freedom—self-pacing only or self-determination of goals and procedures,
• kind of learning guides or clues to be provided for the child's learning procedures,
• ways resources and guides will be made accessible to learners (see #10 and #11).
  Teachers, individually or together,
• prepare learning guides (research questions, clues for choosing among alternative activities in working toward specific goals, step-by-step procedure for a specific activity, etc.)
• collect resources and supplies and arrange them for the learners' use.

During the class session, teachers function as helpers in goal determination, clarifiers of instructions, assistants in locating resources, listeners to children's ideas, participants in child-directed activity, co-participants with children.

Individualized learning ranges from highly structured procedures with children moving individually step by step at their own speed (possibly using programmed resources) to very unstructured individual goal-setting and procedures.

Evaluation centers primarily on individual goal achievement and on progress in self-direction. Relationships of the learner to other learners and to teacher(s) are also included. The child is the evaluator, the teacher a consultant or guide.

A major concern for some teachers is that this approach, with its emphasis on individual learning, might neglect growth in interpersonal relationships, which is an important part of living and learning as Christians. Some of the activities designed for individual initiative can require cooperation of two or more persons for implementation, while others allow more independent action.

This approach requires more preliminary work than some teachers feel capable of, or are willing to do. For these teachers some individualization may be planned in relation to specific needs of the children within a teacher-directed or group-directed situation. Some teachers may find their interest and skills developing through limited use of selected individualization procedures. Many teachers using individualization as a major approach find their satisfaction in the child's initiative and progress overbalancing concern with time-consuming teacher preparation.

Programmed instruction, as used in church education, is a form of individualization rather than a distinctive approach. Usually programmed learning is one alternative for individual choice, or is a procedure for individual work in developing particular skills or exploring content of special interest.

Programmed learning guides are most often guide sheets or books for step-by-step movement toward very specific goals. Guides include self-checking and self-correcting procedures.

Some self-instruction books using programmed steps are available. The Getting to Know Your Bible series[3] is a valuable set for developing skills in using the Bible and for acquiring important information about the Bible. Each child uses the selected book in self-instruction: reading, writing answers, checking answers before moving to the next step—progressing at his or her own pace.

9. Independent study.

The *focus* is on an *individually initiated or accepted plan* for inquiry-discovery learning. It may vary from one special assignment to a total study plan with an overall goal and related learning activities. Some types of independent study are:
• working on selected assignments with research-report procedures (e.g., Christmas customs in different countries, biographical studies, studies of different books of the Bible);
• using independent study guides—selecting which guides to use, choosing among suggested activities, following instructions or making adaptations for own study procedures,
• taking an idea (goal, topic, resource) and developing own approach for exploring or developing that idea.

Independent study as an overall approach is being used by an increasing number of churches in summer when attendance is irregular and there is high interest in change of procedures of ongoing classes. A frequently used plan centers in guided use of a student book and Bible at home as well as in a learning center at the church. Guide sheets prepared by teachers (or writing teams) may be used by the child in whatever order he or she chooses, with freedom of selection among activities described on each sheet. The child usually has a cloth bag or a folder for carrying the book of guide sheets, the student book, and a Bible to and from the church and wherever he or she goes.

Some churches use similar independent study programs throughout the year, in vacation school, or in outdoor education activities.

Teachers in other churches provide a series of guide sheets and a variety of resources and work materials for the children to choose from within the study setting. The resources may be available in a resource library (for the class or for more than one class) and in a supply area, or both study and work materials may be included in centers for learning in the classroom.

LEARNING CENTER APPROACH[4]

- Centers (areas) for learning may be corners, rooms, alcoves, movable units, a whole house or a group of rooms.
- Each learner chooses the center in which he or she will use available resources and activities for inquiry-discovery learning and for expression of personal insights and feelings.
- The individual decides when to move from one center to another, and when to move out into other parts of the church or into the community for extending his or her area for inquiry-exploration or service.
- Teachers function as resource providers, guide developers, facilitators, enablers, consultants, resource persons, and such.

10. **Learning center approach—different forms.**

The *focus* in the learning center approach is on the *way of making related learning resources available* in centers *for independent use* by individual learners or groups of learners.

The *learning center approach* in the church school may be used by a single teacher but is more often used by a teaching team. The way of learning is *self-directed* study, exploration, expression.

Centers for learning may be used in unit teaching (approaches #3 and #4) or in group teaching (#5). In these situations the centers are generally interest centers used for a limited portion of the class time. These interest centers are designed for motivation or for expressional activities related to teacher-directed or group-directed study.

The learning center, as an overall approach in the church school, includes a number of centers for individual or small-group inquiry-discovery learning. (see approaches #8 and #9.) Each center is a self-contained area with resources for individual use in working toward specific goals. A center may be as small as the end of a church pew or a corner of a rug. It may be as large as a whole pew or rug, or even larger.

Teachers usually use regular church-school curriculum units as primary resources for designing centers related to the unit goals. Some teachers develop their own unit—determining goals and collecting appropriate resources for the centers they plan to use.

The teaching team, or the single teacher, determines
- the unit purpose and specific learning goals;
- learning needs—content, experiences;
- activities for self-directed use;
- ways the goals, content, and activities can be brought together in centers for learning;
- how centers will be designed—
   —as content centers (different portions of the unit content) with a variety of activities in each center for exploring that content, or
   —as activity centers (music, research, art, drama, etc.) with varied or overlapping content.

With these decisions made, teachers together or individual teachers design each center with its own
- learning goal(s),
- content,
- resources (student books, other books, Bible(s), pictures, audiovisuals, objects, construction materials…)
- guide(s) for self-directed use of the center resources.

Each center is designed with one goal or several goals. A particular center may have one activity or only one or two basic resources, or it may offer a choice of activities and/or resources.

The teacher(s) in developing a center, or centers, considers:
• the age level (or levels) of the learners and their capabilities and interests;
• possible activities for the less mature and more mature learners, and for those whose learning is strengthened through words, visuals, or action;
• ways of designing the center to invite the children's interest and initiative.

The child selects the center in which he or she will begin. The decision may be interest-oriented or goal-directed. The time spent in a particular center will depend on
• the child's goal (self-determined or chosen from goals suggested by the teacher),
• the extent of the child's interest in the content and activities of the area (center),
• the time required for completion of the selected activities.

Guides (questions, charts, guidesheets) for the center help children know
• what goal(s) may be achieved in the center,
• what steps are to be taken or what alternative activities may be chosen,
• what is to be completed before moving to another center.

Each child makes her or his own decisions and directs her/his own learning activities. Teachers are available as supporters, encouragers, listeners, resource persons, co-learners, enablers.

Two major concerns related to the learning center approach are
• content coverage,
• interpersonal relationships.

Many teachers have found they have more person-to-person relationships with individual students in this teaching-learning approach than in some other approaches. With goals, resources, and centers ready for child use, the teacher is free to serve as consultant, friend, guide, responder. Some teachers design centers, or specific activities, for involvement of the child with other children. These teachers often find that children will take the initiative in relating to one another in shared use of resources and in working together on common interests.

The illustration in chapter 8 of the group using the learning-center approach (group 3) showed that children can be very excited about the learning procedures in the learning center and at the same time deal responsibly with the content being explored. The design of the centers, the clarity of goals, and the appropriateness of resources and activities are all important in creation of exciting, effective learning experiences.

The student evaluates his or her use of a center in terms of discoveries made, activities used, goals achieved. The teacher evaluates in terms of the children's overall involvement, and in terms of usability of guides and resources for different children in working toward the selected goals.

11. **Learning Center Approach—Open Classroom.**
The *focus* in open classroom education is on *freedom* of the learner—*to be, to do, to learn.*
Openness in the classroom may be in
• room arrangement with all centers for learning easily visible for ease in choice and movement,
• individual freedom of movement from one learning area to another,
• attitude of openness among leaders and learners; a freedom in relationships as well as in use of resources,
Open education, or the open classroom as an approach in church education, is *a philsosphy of teaching-learning* characterized by
• honest, open relationships among leaders and learners,
• fostering of child's sense of self-worth
• mutual respect and valuing of other persons' ideas and insights.

Teacher (teaching team) planning includes attention to
• curriculum content with its possibilities for emotional, social, physical, and intellectual learning—growth for the whole child,
• learning environment—total area, centers, resources, and guides—for freeing the child to be himself or herself in interaction with resources, other children, and leaders.

An open classroom in terms of use of space and organization of resources is not equivalent to open-classroom education. This type of classroom environment, however, does offer a setting in which teachers and children can participate in open education. The open-classroom setting contributes to a climate in which the child may
• move about with ease, relating freely with other learners and with leaders;
• experience herself or himself as a valued, trusted person;

- share thoughts as well as resources;
- find acceptance and respect from teachers and other students;
- explore ways of learning of his or her own choosing;
- use resources of his or her own selection;
- work toward self-determined or selected goals.

The open classroom, then, is one that might be described as a nurturing community. Leaders and learners are members together in this community, sharing their faith, their interests, their feelings, their insights in the context of an exploration-discovery setting.

A major concern of teachers considering open classroom education is the possible loss of control—whether there will be responsible freedom or chaos. Relinquishing the security of authority can be threatening to both child and teacher. Many teachers find that they and the children need time to experiment with and adjust to new ways of working and of relating to one another.

Teachers, uneasy about attempting an open classroom, might first try allowing children more limited choice and self-direction for short-term interest activities or projects.

CONTRACTING

Contracting may be for
- a particular assignment or responsibility,
- participation in a special study setting for a stated time (e.g., a short-term intergenerational class),
- completion of an agreed upon plan for working on personal or group learning goals,

12. A contract approach.

The *focus* is on *two-way agreement between learners and leaders.*

A contract may be used in almost any teaching-learning approach. In a predominantly teacher-directed class the agreement is more likely to be the students' acceptance of an assignment with the teacher promising to remind the student before the assignment is due. In a group-directed class, members of the group may covenant with one another to work toward agreed upon goals, or to accept individual or committee responsibility for certain areas of work within the total group learning plan.

Contract learning, as an approach now in use in some churches, utilizes an independent study plan (approach #9) or some other form of individualized learning or learning-center design (approaches #8, #10, or #11). The *intent* of the contract, *who* contracts, and the *agreements* included are determined by the local church designers—a teaching team or a committee.

Persons contracting may be learners and leaders, or may be children and their parents with teachers and church administrators. In the latter case, the contract, or covenant, includes
- the children's commitment, with parental support, to goals to be achieved and the time and effort to be committed,
- the teacher's or teaching team's commitment, with backing of church officials, to provision of resources and guidance.

Teacher preparation, in consultation with children and their parents, might include determination of
- group or individual goals,
- kinds of child involvement anticipated: hours or sessions, kinds of work or activities to be completed,
- teacher involvement: how to support child, how to provide resources,
- plan for evaluation.

Class session procedures would be determined according to the agreement—committee work, independent study, sharing in total group from individual or small group research or other activities.

Contracting is generally more a matter of commitment or covenanting than a definable teaching-learning approach. It is being used, however, as the framework, or approach, within which other forms of teaching-learning take on new importance and vitality.

In this chapter, we have reviewed twelve learning approaches used in church education with children—in peer or intergenerational groups. We have seen that each approach has unique characteristics, but procedures typical of one approach may sometimes be used also in other approaches. In the illustrations at the beginning of chapter 8, we noted that similar learning activities are used in different general teaching-learning approaches.

The teacher (teaching team) determines, or involves class members in deciding, the approach the class will use—throughout the year or for a given period of time. The approach chosen and developed may be
• an approach described in this chapter,
• a variation of one of these approaches,
• an approach different from any of the ones described,
• a hybrid of two or more of these general approaches.

Reread the sentences you completed on page 70 for identifying your approach with your class. Do those sentences adequately describe your teaching-learning approach? If not, write a new brief description. Use ideas from any of the preceeding descriptions that are appropriate. Include ideas on your focus in planning and on teacher and student involvement in class sessions that you feel characterize your preparation and your class procedures.

_____
_____
_____
_____

Note any characteristics of other approaches that appeal to you as being worthy of your consideration.

_____
_____
_____
_____

In chapter 11 we bring together some thoughts on evaluation of teaching-learning as clues to more effective teaching. In the latter part of the chapter we evaluate principles for use in determining an overall approach in the church-school class.

EVALUATING TEACHING-LEARNING EFFECTIVENESS

Evaluation should look ahead to future
work as well as deal with the quality
of any particular effort.[1]

From time to time throughout this book we refer to evaluation as a part of the total process of planning and teaching-learning. The cycle is incomplete if evaluation is omitted. Evaluation is the link between the past and the future. Evaluation brings into perspective experiences of the past—goal achievement, high peak experiences, disappointments, satisfactions, inadequate plans—as clues to more effective planning for the future. The full planning cycle then includes planning . . . teaching-learning . . . evaluating . . . planning . . .

As in other phases of the whole teaching learning process, who does evaluation, what is evaluated, and how evaluation is done is related to
• our understanding of the objective of Christian education and our specific goals;
• our understanding of children, their needs, and how they grow and learn;
• our primary way of teaching-learning: teacher-directed, group-directed, self-directed;
• the approach we are using—which form of session-by-session approach, unit teaching, learning center, or some other.

Basically the whole idea of evaluation is *what do we want to know* and *why*. Questions such as the following can lead to insights as to what is happening in a class, what learning is taking place, and how learning experiences might be strengthened:

What were we trying to teach? Were we primarily concerned with content, concepts, values, behavior, attitudes?

How did I (we) attempt to teach these?

What clues do I (we) have that children learned or changed? What did they learn? How?

What knowledge (information, insights), attitudes, values, skills, behavior were strengthened? What new ones were acquired? How are new ones beginning to develop?

What difficulties did children face in dealing with content, concepts, values? In working individually or with others? How did they handle these difficulties?

What kinds of experiences in the future would be useful to individual children or the group in

(a) exploring ideas, learning information, developing valuing skills;

(b) growing in self-image and self-confidence;

(c) growing in knowledge and experience of God and in response to God's love;

(d) growing in discipleship to Jesus Christ.

Your own questions will be selective and more specific in terms of what you want to know and why.

In *developing evaluation questions and procedures,* first ask, What do I want to know from the evaluation? and How will I (we) use findings from the evaluation in planning other teaching-learning opportunities?

A question often asked about learning-center or open-classroom approaches is, How can we know if children are learning? The same question should be asked of any learning situation. What clues do you look for—verbal? body language? attitudes? enthusiasm or lack of it? What else?

The question, How can we know if children are learning? must be preceded by, What do we anticipate that children should/will learn? Are we concerned with facts, concepts, ability to evaluate and act? Then, How can we know if (or when) the children have learned or are learning?

What were the goals for learning? Are we seeking individual achievement? Group goals? Individual involvement in group life?

Who formulated the goals? The teacher? The children? The group? Are these sets of goals the same? Interrelated? In conflict? Correlated? Unrelated?

Ask not only, What have they learned? but also, What are the indicators that they are learning?—relationships with one another, handling of tasks, responsiveness in worship . . .

Are we looking for "right answers" or evidence that the child is learning how to deal with valuing situations? Do we emphasize "right answers" or an understanding of issues and how to reach solutions? Is our concern with knowledge and/or life?

Has there been a balance of independent and interdependent learning opportunities? What balance am I trying to achieve? How do independence or interdependence relate to achievement of goals for the class?

How are occasional attenders involved in learning activities? How does their irregular attendance affect more regular attenders? What are the teacher expectations for regular and irregular attenders? Are these expectations realistic? Does a high rate of inconsistent attendance necessitate a week-by-week self-contained lesson rather than unit planning that will continue over several weeks? In what ways can poor attenders be involved in activities and content?

Did some children complete activities quicker than others? Why? How were children encouraged and reinforced to learn at their own pace? Is it ever possible or advisable to keep all learners moving at same pace? What activities, if any, require total group participation? Which are more appropriate for individuals or small groups?

How much self-direction was observed in the children's approach in learning? How much teacher-direction was provided? Were there times when less or more teacher help was needed? To what extent did the teacher help or encourage individual children according to their varying capabilities?

How were children involved in action-reflection learning? Were they able to recall and reflect on out-of-class experiences and to explore alternative solutions or value decisions? Are they ready for this kind of thinking and decision-making?

Curriculum units generally include some guidance on evaluation—both on what to evaluate and on possible evaluation questions or procedures. In some units, evaluation is centered on progress toward goals over a full unit or several sessions of related learning experiences. Some units include also session-by-session evaluation ideas. The assumptions about learners and learning and about goals will influence the kind of evaluation guidance given. (See chapter 8 for ideas on curriculum series and use of curriculum units.)

Many of the exercises throughout this book are evaluative, with the focus on your own (and my own) teaching-learning styles and procedures. This is especially true in chapter 7, "Inventing Your Own Style of Teaching." Self-improvement is possible for each of us as individual teachers or teaching teams. Improvement in teaching-learning in any situation is also possible.

In chapter 6, we suggest that the main focus of evaluation for any group is related to the way of teaching-learning used: teacher-directed, group-directed, or self-directed. In chapters 5 and 6 we note the relationship between those who do the evaluation, the primary way of teaching-learning, and those who make major decisions.

For teacher-directed learning, the main focus of evaluation is on the child's ability to store and retrieve information as given by teacher(s) or processed by the child. Leaders are the evaluators of goal achievement, procedures, and learner behavior, possibly getting feedback from the children on what they have learned or on procedure preferences.

For group-directed learning, evaluation is related to group goal achievement and group members' ability to use data out of inquiry learning and group process. Leaders and learners together are the evaluators of goal achievement, group processes, and working relationships in group, possibly including also evaluation of ways of meeting individual needs.

For self-directed learning, evaluation centers in individual goal achievement and on ability of individuals to process and use data from inquiry and from own working procedures and relationships. The child, in consultation with a leader (leaders), evaluates his or her own goal achievement, choice and pacing of activities, and his or her own relationships with other persons.

Describing your present teaching approach and noting characteristics of other approaches that appeal to you as being worthy of your consideration is a step in evaluation. (See chapter 10, especially page 80.)

Your decision to change or to stick with your present approach may be simply "This looks better to me"; or "I feel my present approach is OK." In evaluating your general approach you are concerned, as in other kinds of evaluation, with observed goal achievement (or lack of achievement) and clues as to what learning has taken place. You are further concerned with whether

• your present approach provides for involving children in effective learning experiences,
• your approach needs strengthening or revamping,
• some other approach offers better potential for the immediate future.

In the descriptions of teaching-learning approaches (chapter 10), we identify

• major focus in teacher planning (content, teacher action, child involvement, procedures),
• teacher responsibilities in class session,
• child involvement in the learning experience.

These are factors you will question as you consider validity and potential effectiveness of a particular approach for your own class.

Further, we note specific concerns some teachers have in relation to certain approaches. Your feelings about these concerns (agreement, disagreement, uncertainty) and your thoughts on how to deal with them and other concerns of your own are part of your evaluation of your present approach or your consideration of an alternative approach.

For a more adequate assessment of alternative approaches, ways of teaching-learning, and teaching styles, it might help to examine the principles or motivations influencing some teachers' decisions.

PRINCIPLES OR MOTIVATIONS

1. Read through the entire list of principles. Restate some and add others, if you so desire.
2. Check (√) on the left those *principles by which you have been most influenced.* Check from one to three or four—more if you wish.
3. On the right rank each principle (entire list) according to *how important you feel it should be in your teaching-learning decisions.*
4. To what extent do your most influential principles coincide with those you now view as very important or important?

Very Important   Important   Unimportant   Undesirable

Availability. Resources required are on hand or easily available.

Balance. Child involvement in activities and learning of content are to be kept in balance.

Biblical focus. Bible and life must be brought together.

Child-centered. I teach children. Goals and content are for them.

Commitment. Commitment to Christ and his church is a primary goal in all Christian education.

Community, fellowship. The school of the church is a place for experiencing the feeling of belonging in the Christian community and for growing and learning in the Christian fellowship.

Communication. learning by the child is dependent on adequacy of communication: two-way between child and teacher and interchange among children and teacher(s).

Curriculum direction. My curriculum materials tell me just what to teach, and I follow this step by step.

Evaluation. Evaluation of previous procedures and goal attainment are basic to future planning.

Flexibility. For effective teaching-learning experiences, plans must include openness to modification or adaptation as teacher(s) and children work together.

Goal-directed. Goals are basic for setting directions (content and procedures) for learning and for assessing progress or achievement.

Group life. Relationships among group members are important as both goal and process in Christian education.

Heritage. The church has a heritage of faith, a history rooted in the Bible, which is a basic foundation for the learner's own faith and commitment.

Humanization. Teaching-learning experiences in the church should help each person attain his or her greatest human potential as a person created by God.

Individualization. Teaching-learning plans must be geared to needs and interests of the individual child.

Imitation. My favorite teacher taught this way.

Innovation. New or novel ways of teaching are necessary for gaining and holding children's attention.

Integration. Teaching-learning procedures must be in harmony with the content being taught—providing an integrated whole of goals, content, and procedures.

Motivation. Learners must have desire or stimulation for becoming involved with content and learning procedures.

Support, affirmation. Children learn best when they sense that the teacher feels they are persons of worth and are capable of handling the content and procedures of their own learning experiences.

Tradition. This has always been the way teaching in my church is done. Procedures of the past are what we need for the present.

Transmission. Instructing children in the Bible and the Christian heritage is the purpose of church-school teaching. The church has a faith, a content to transmit from one generation to the next.

_____ **Variety.** Variety is necessary for enabling children to utilize their own
varied interests and capabilities for learning.   _____ _____ _____ _____

_____

From reviewing and checking the above statements:
(a) I learned that I _____
_____

(b) I find that I need to give more attention to _____
_____
_____

You have been looking at your present teaching style, ways of teaching-learning, and approach in education in terms of your own motivation. The next step in evaluation is to look to the future. What difference will this assessment make in your future plans and procedures?

Describe below your intentions for the immediate future with your class. You may vary at other times.

My *purposes* in teaching are (copied or revised from #3, pages 49-50):_____
_____
_____ .

My *goals* for my class for the immediate future are (see chapter 3, pages 20-21, and the suggested goals in your next curriculum unit): _____
_____
_____

My *way of teaching-learning* will be primarily the one checked below (see chapters 5 and 6):
        _____ teacher-directed
        _____ group-directed
        _____ self-directed
because I feel it is important that the children _____
_____
_____

My responsibilities as teacher will be (see chapter 7, especially your checked or written statement on pages 51-52):_____
_____
_____

Members of my class will be involved in learning through use of these activities (see chapter 9): _____
_____

The teaching-learning approach for my class will be (see chapter 10, especially your own statements on pages 70 and 80):_____
_____

As you continue evaluating and reevaluating your ways of teaching-learning, your style of relating to members of your class, and your approach(es) in church education, may you find increasingly effective ways of enabling children
—to know and respond to God's love,
—to experience what it means to be a disciple of Jesus Christ, a Christian,
—to live a Christian life in day-by-day relationships, empowered by the Holy Spirit.

CONTINUING TEACHER EXPLORATION AND GROWTH

12

OBSERVATIONS ABOUT LEARNING AND TEACHING

This chapter offers a summary of ideas on teaching and learning that are more fully developed in other chapters of this book. The number(s) in parentheses ( ) with each statement refers to the chapter(s) providing further development of the idea.

Your reactions to observations included below will help bring into focus your own present perceptions as a teacher/leader in church education. You may wish to respond to each observation, or you may prefer to check only those statements which particularly catch your attention. Revise or add statements, if you so desire, to make the checked statements reflect more nearly your own thoughts.

✦

Respond to any or all of the following ideas by checking on the right whether you *agree, disagree,* or are *uncertain* (question the meaning or validity of a statement).

If you agree, put a check (√) in the first column.
If you disagree, put a check (√) in the second column.
If you are uncertain about the meaning of a statement or question the validity of the idea, put a question mark (?) in the third column.

	Agree	Disagree	Uncertain
The objective of Christian education is that each person know and respond to God's love, be a committed Christian, and fulfill his or her Christian discipleship. (2, 3)	—	—	—
Christian education includes all experiences (in home, church, elsewhere) that enable a person to grow in knowledge and love of God and in commitment to Jesus Christ. (1)	—	—	—
The church school provides for planned teaching-learning experiences for developing Christians. (1)	—	—	—
The church school includes Sunday school and other study and informal teaching-learning settings. (1)	—	—	—
Christian education in the coming years must include not only instruction in the heritage of the Christian faith but also guidance for living in an uncertain present and future. (3)	—	—	—
Learning is personal, individual. Christian experience and life is unique for each person. (3)	—	—	—

The individual is responsible for (in control of) his or her own learning. (4)   ___ ___ ___

Each child's readiness for particular learning experiences is interrelated with the stage of development in the whole of that child's living and learning. (4)   ___ ___ ___

Each person responds to the Christian gospel with his or her own degree of commitment, expressed in that person's own life and witness as a disciple of Jesus Christ. (3)   ___ ___ ___

There is a difference in "knowing about" and "knowing." Christian commitment includes knowing, being, and doing. (4)   ___ ___ ___

A person learns in interaction with other persons, resources, experiences. (5)   ___ ___ ___

The learner needs both independent, self-directed learning opportunities, and interchange of ideas and perceptions with other persons for developing and testing knowledge, skills, understandings, values, attitudes. (5)   ___ ___ ___

Each child (or older person) has strengths and limitations in learning capabilities. (4) Some persons are more
—visual, verbal, or action-oriented in their most effective ways of learning;
—independent, interdependent, or dependent in their approaches in learning;
—inclined toward learning procedures that are easier for them or that are challenging to their thoughts and skills.   ___ ___

Effective teaching-learning can take place in teacher-directed, group-directed, or self-directed ways of learning. (5, 6)   ___ ___

Teachers can be creative, individually or in a teaching team, in ways of teaching-learning and in adaptation or combination of varied approaches in church education. (6, 9, 10)   ___ ___ ___

Teaching style is a combination of the teacher's or teaching team's attitudes, actions, and relationships in the teaching-learning situation. (7)   ___ ___ ___

The teacher (team) determines the teaching style used in a particular class—a unique style for that teacher (team). (7)   ___ ___ ___

Local church teachers use a variety of teaching styles and education approaches. Styles and approaches of long history and of recent development are currently in use. (7, 10)   ___ ___ ___

Curriculum materials for the church school are tools, guides, resources for leaders and learners. (8)   ___ ___ ___

Any curriculum material may be used as a basic resource in preparing for teacher-directed, group-directed, or self-directed learning. (5, 8)   ___ ___ ___

A teacher (or team) can use any curriculum material for any desired educational approach by adaptation through selecting, expanding, supplementing goals, ideas, and procedures. (8, 10)   ___ ___ ___

The total teaching-learning process includes a continuous cycle of planning . . . teaching-learning . . . evaluating . . . planning . . . (6, 11)   ___ ___ ___

Evaluation includes assessment of goal achievement, peak experiences, disappointments, failures, successes, procedures contributing or not contributing to goal achievement, personal and group relationships, evidences of learning achieved. (11)   ___ ___ ___

Evaluation links prior experience with future planning as teachers seek to provide for more effective teaching-learning. (11)   ___ ___ ___

Look back over the statements above—those with which you agree or disagree, and those you question. Complete one or more of the following sentences.

In reviewing my checking or questioning of the above summary ideas I see that I _____
_____ .

Some of my own views on ideas with which I disagree are _____
_____ .

I would like to do further study in relation to _____
_____ .

Star (*) ideas below and on the following pages that merit special consideration as you plan for and work with your class.

_____ Roles and relationships of teachers and learners vary in different groups, or in the same group at different times. (7, 10)

Teachers may	and	learners may
• give information		• accept/reject/ignore information
• provide resources		• use resources for exploration or pass over those resources lightly
• direct process or guide learners in developing process		• participate as directed, rebel against process, challenge and influence process
• function as co-learner		• help determine learning goals as well as procedures
• be primarily a teacher but also a student		• function as contributing students, teaching as well as learning
• be the evaluator, or guide learners in evaluation		• evaluate own progress toward goals or participate in group evaluation.

_____ Distinctions in ways of learning and teaching (teacher-directed, group-directed, self-directed) may be made in terms of who makes major decisions. (5, 6)

_____ Decisions may be made by
• teacher(s) as leader (teaching team),
• teacher(s) and students as leader-learners,
• students with teacher(s) as learners together,
• individual student(s) as learner(s) with teacher guidance.

_____ The teacher (teaching team) determines the extent to which learners are involved in decision-making in any or all parts of the learning process (6):
• goal-setting
• selection of resources
• determination of activities, procedures
• pacing of work
• evaluation

_____ The range of learner decisions varies widely. (6) It may
• be as limited as choice of color for an outlined picture in the child's book or choice between two specified activities; or
• be as inclusive as full participation in determining study theme, goals, general approach, specific methods, pacing of work, choice of the child's way of contributing to group determined plans or of pursuing individual goals, evaluation of goal achievement, individual participation and group process.

_____ Learner decision-making may be anywhere on this continuum (6)

single choice	interest group	involvement in
decisions	decisions	all decisions

_____ The general approach of a teacher (team) and class may be identified by three key characteristics (10):
• major focus in teacher planning (one or more of the following: content, class procedures, unit or session purposes, teacher and learner roles and relationships, selection and organization of resources);

- in-class roles and responsibilities of teacher(s);
- ways children are involved in learning.

—— The learning approach of a class may be (10)
- a well-identified single approach (e.g., project development and implementation);
- a variation of a general approach (e.g., community building form of learning center approach);
- a combination of approaches (e.g., group teaching moving to a committee-class approach or group development of learning centers).

—— The learning approach used by a class may be determined in a variety of ways. (10) It may be
- determined in advance by teacher or teaching team,
- decided by the class with teacher guidance,
- developed by class and teacher(s) together in group decision-making.

—— Teacher-direction, group teaching, and individualized learning are not necessarily mutually exclusive teaching-learning procedures. (6, 10)
- Teacher directed learning may allow for some individual or group determination of activities or their implementation.
- Group teaching may include consideration of individual interests and/or allow for individual initiative/implementation of ideas or plans related to group projects.
- Individualized learning may include learning procedures necessitating or allowing for interaction with other learners.

—— Many factors are involved in determining teaching style and learning approaches (7, 10). Some of these factors are:
- age or grade level(s) of children in learning group;
- overall objective of Christian education, teacher's (team's) purposes in teaching, and goals / theme / focus of unit currently being used;
- teacher's or team's previous experience and/or openness to risk of change, individual or collective capabilities, willingness of leaders to learn new skills.

—— *Teacher-directed* learning may be (6)
- entirely teacher-directed with all students following teacher instructions, for total group, small groups, or individual work toward teacher-determined goals;
- teacher-directed in goal determination and selection of resources and activities, with some student freedom in choice of certain types of activities (e.g., interest groups chosen by students from among alternatives provided by the teacher);
- teacher-directed in involving individuals or the group in some decision-making within the boundaries determined by the teacher or teaching team.

—— *Team teaching* may involve teaming (10)
- in teacher planning, with assigned or chosen individual teacher responsibilities for implementation in teaching;
- in cooperative teaching as well as planning, with supportiveness in implementation of individual and corporate responsibilities;
- in preparation for and implementation of teacher-directed learning, group teaching, or individualized instruction.

—— *Group process* may involve learners in (10)
- leader-directed problem-solving,
- group-directed planning with group members assuming various roles of group maintenance,
- procedures for involving group members in teaching-learning activities,
- group participation in goal-setting, planning, action, evaluation.

—— *Group teaching* may
- subordinate the individual and his or her needs and interests to wishes of the majority, or
- take account of and make provision for individual concerns, interests,
- be guided by a single teacher or a teaching team. (10)

—— *A unit approach*
- coordinates goals, activities, projects for a series of sessions on one theme or focus,

    • allows for more flexibility, variety, continuity, and relatedness of dealing with content and procedures than does a single-session approach. (10, 8)

—— *Independent study* (10) may be
    • self-directed or teacher-guided,
    • isolated individual study or individual choice of activities involving working alone and/or with others.

—— *Individualization* (10) may be in any one or a combination of the following:
    • setting or selection of one's own learning goals,
    • working at own pace, using programmed guides in sequence,
    • selecting learning content and/or procedures in order of one's own choosing.

—— *Individualization* (10) may be anywhere on a continuum

completely self-directed				highly structured
self-initiated				programmed by leader

—— *Centers for learning* (10) may be
    • interest centers used for a limited time by individuals or small groups for exploring or expressing ideas being developed in total group study (teacher- or group-directed), or
    • learning centers designed for individual or small-group use as the major learning approach in self-directed study, exploration, expression of ideas.

—— *Learning Centers* (10) may be organized around
    • areas of content with a variety of activities in each area (e.g., an area on Moses in a study of early heroes of the faith, with activities involving research, drama, art);
    • types of exploration areas with varied activities in each area (e.g., archaeology or research areas with activities in each area requiring use of Bible, use of student book, some expression in art or in writing of responses by learner);
    • interest areas (music, art, use of books, drama, etc.) using theme-related content in each area.

—— *Open classroom* (10) may be any or all of the following:
    • openness in arrangement of room—visibility of all learning areas, free availability of all resources;
    • openness in freedom of individuals to choose when, where, what each will do;
    • openness in atmosphere and in attitude of participants, both leaders and learners;
    • openness within limits—freedom within boundaries.

—— *Intergenerational learning* (10) experiences
    • involve two or more generations (children, youth, adults) in learning together;
    • may be study, action, worship, fellowship, with active group member interchange in process and ideas;
    • focus on persons of different generations learning from and with one another (as distinct from persons of one generation teaching learners of another generation).

—— The Bible, church heritage, Christian life may all be taught and learned at three different levels (4), each of which is important in Christian education:
    • fact—information, what happened;
    • concept—meaning, message, implications, affirmation of beliefs, views;
    • valuing or decision-making—response, commitment, action.

—— Being and becoming Christian, for both learner and leader, is personal. Each person is involved in maturing as a Christian—in knowing, being, acting in response to God's love and will, in degree of commitment to Jesus Christ, and in acceptance of guidance of the Holy Spirit. (3, 7)

—— The spiritual life of an individual involves
    • feelings about self, other persons, God;
    • responses to God, to Jesus Christ, to the Holy Spirit;
    • responses to other persons and to the natural world. (5)

—— The church is concerned with the child's (older person's) spiritual growth within the individual's total life development and in all that person's relationships with God, Jesus Christ, Holy Spirit, and with self, other persons, and the natural world. (4, 5)

Select one idea that you starred in the preceding statements. Note here how you intend to use that idea in planning or in teaching.

_____

_____

We, who are teachers
in the church school
have responded
to
Jesus' call to
"Go—teach!"
In our teaching
we seek to fulfill
the church's objective
that
each person know and respond to
the love of God
as
revealed in Jesus Christ.
Methods, materials,
ways of teaching and learning
are means of
enabling children and older persons
to
know themselves as children of God,
responding in discipleship to Jesus Christ,
living in Christian commitment,
through the empowerment of the Holy Spirit.

Growing, learning, teaching can be exciting, fun, taking us into deep thoughts and exhilarating insights, new relationships or discovery of new meaning in old relationships, challenging us to new commitments or re-dedication to old commitments.

Growing, learning, teaching can also involve growing pains, hard work, struggles with feelings, thoughts, concerns, attitudes.

In prayer, study, meditation, support, and counsel from other persons, insights from church-school resources, we find power and understanding for utilizing high and low moments, strengths and limitations for growth as Christians and as leaders in church education.

As you continue your own venture in learning and teaching, you may want to

a) use your own check marks (√), questions (?), or stars(*) in this chapter to direct you to earlier chapters for further exploration;

b) use chapter 13 or a system of your own for outlining your continuing personal growth plan;

c) select from the bibliography a resource or two for a next step in digging deeper in an area of immediate interest.

13
THE GROWING TEACHER

Self-Insight
Self-Affirmation
Self-Improvement

Stop   see the children
Look   hear them
Listen   learn from
         the children

Study   biblical and
Meditate   theological
Pray   dimensions
        of faith

Adopt   goals
or   ideas
Adapt   procedures
        use of resources

The more we learn the more we realize there is more to learn.

Explore   ways of teaching
Experiment   learning
Evaluate   approaches in learning

Affirm   personal beliefs
Revise   perceptions of children
Change   views on teaching
        and learning

Innovate   ideas
Renovate   methods
Create   approaches
        settings for
        learning

Throughout this book we have been
—reflecting on our own growing, learning, teaching experiences,
—exploring and assessing ways of teaching and learning and various approaches in church education,
—anticipating, looking ahead to the future in Christian education and how we might influence its effectiveness.

You have been on a venture of learning and growing throughout your life to the present. This venture continues—planned or unplanned.

Ideas in this chapter, or similar ones of your own, may help you in being more intentional about your next steps in continuing growth as a teacher or other leader in the church school.

Make a contract with yourself!

(a) Write your own
     "I will _____" commitment.
                                         or

(b) Check and fill in one or more ideas below that you intend to pursue.

GENERAL IMPROVEMENT AS A TEACHER

☐ As I have thought of my own growing-up experiences and of my more recent experiences in learning and teaching, I observe that I _____ .

In my own teaching experiences, I feel good about_____

_____ .

From my reflection and related study, I will try to become a better teacher by _____

_____

_____ .

☐ In the experiences / learnings of members of my class, I am satisfied or pleased about _____

_____ . We could improve our teaching-learning together in_____

_____ .

I will try to bring this about by _____

_____

_____ .

☐ I will seek counsel from or share and explore ideas with another teacher, a counseling teacher, an administrator, a friend.

A person from whom I can seek counsel is _____

A person (same or different) with whom I can share mutual concerns and explore ideas is _____

_____ .

WORKING WITH MEMBERS OF MY CLASS

☐ I will try to improve my ways of working with boys and girls in my class by _____

_____ .

☐ In the next session or within the next unit, I will select from my curriculum material for use with my class at least one activity I have not used recently or ever. Some possibilities are: _____   _____

_____   _____

_____   _____

☐ In order to achieve the following goal or purpose in the next class session or unit, _____

(goal or purpose)

_____

_____," I will plan for (with) my class to _____

_____ .

☐ In the next _____ I will experiment with a different approach in teaching-learning

(unit, month, quarter)

with my (our) class. An approach I feel is appropriate for my class and for this particular study is

_____ .

☐ As I relate to the children, I will be more intentional in

_____ .

GROWTH THROUGH READING, STUDY, MEDITATION

☐ By _____ I will have read, reviewed, studied, at least one of the resources I am listing

(date)

below (from the bibliography, page 95, from suggestions in curriculum materials, from suggestions of a friend, from some other source)

_____

_____

_____

_____

As I complete a resource, I will check it above.

☐ For the next _____ weeks I will study seriously the biblical and theological background material in my teacher book.

☐ I will spend at least an average of _____ hours per week in preparation for my class sessions.

PARTICIPATION IN TRAINING OR ENRICHMENT PROGRAMS

☐ I will discover what local church or area events are scheduled for faith enrichment, biblical or theological study, study of teaching-learning procedures. Events in which I am interested are:

event	place	date	schedule

I will attend the event(s) starred (*) above.

PERSONAL SPIRITUAL DEVELOPMENT

☐ I will continue, or begin, participation in the following worship or spiritual enrichment program(s) of my own church or in my community:

_____

_____

_____

☐ My personal spiritual life can be strengthened through private prayer, reading of books designed for spiritual enrichment, family devotionals. Within the coming _____
(week, month, year)

I will _____

_____

_____ .

> Blessed are you when your church says, "teach our children," for then are you numbered among those who follow the great command, "Go . . . teach!" . . . For as you teach you also will learn and grow.[1]

NOTES

INTRODUCTION

1. For similar ideas on life-span development (children-youth-adults) refer to George Koehler, *Learning Together: A Guide for Intergenerational Education in the Church* (Nashville: Discipleship Resources, 1977), pp. 35-44.

2. Apparently he was referring to a chapter on intergenerational learning in my book *Vacation Time—Leisure Time—Any Time You Choose* (Nashville: Abingdon, 1974).

1. LEARNING AND TEACHING IN THE CHURCH

1. Adapted from a paper, "Guidelines for Education," by Howard M. Ham.

2. From *Design for United Methodist Curriculum* (Nashville: Graded Press, 1969), p. 11. The Cooperative Curriculum Project statement of objective is given on page 17.

3. Adapted from Mary Alice Jones, *The Christian Faith Speaks to Children* (Nashville: Abingdon, 1965), p. 40.

4. Quoted phrases from W. E. Dugger, Jr., "Christ and Human Liberty," devotional reading for July 4, 1976, in The Upper Room Disciplines (Nashville: The Upper Room, 1976).

2. LOOK BACK TO LOOK AHEAD

1. Dr. Marion Brown, St. Paul School of Theology Kansas City, Missouri, worked with me in designing and resourcing my self-directed study. Early in my study, a book outline became a way of organizing and testing my developing insights.

2. For more on the history of the church school, see Paul H. Vieth, "Christian Education—Yesterday and Today," chapter 1 in *The Church and Christian Education* (St. Louis: Bethany Press, 1947). According to Dr. Vieth and others, the origin of the Sunday school is usually set at 1780. Robert Raikes, concerned about the "ragged, dirty, profane, delinquent, underprivileged, ignorant" children of his city, gathered these children together for education. Sunday was the day, for the children were then free from work. As public schools later assumed more responsibility for general education for all children, church schools directed their program more to religious education, with strong emphasis on Bible teaching and memorization.

3. This statement of aims is adapted from chapter 2 of W. C. Bower's *Religious Education in the Modern Church* (St Louis: Bethany Press, 1929). In this book the author urges the church to define its objectives in order to develop programs, that will most effectively fulfill the church's educational function.

4. Adapted from Mary E. Skinner, *Children's Work in the Church* (Nashville: Cokesbury Press, 1932), pp. 16-17.

5. This statement and the following areas for Christian nurture are from "Goals for Christian Education of Children," International Council of Religious Education, 1945.

6. From John Q. Schisler, *Christian Teaching in the Churches* (Nashville: Abingdon, 1954), pp. 29-30. Quoting from 1950 Yearbook of the International Council of Religious Education. (Emphasis mine.)

7. From *The Church's Educational Ministry: A Curriculum Plan*, the work of the Cooperative Curriculum Project (St Louis: Bethany Press, 1965), p. 8 (emphasis mine). Available earlier in working papers for use by cooperating denominations in curriculum planning. Fundamental questions and curriculum areas from this same source.

3. CHRISTIAN EDUCATION IN THE COMING YEARS

1. Many ideas in this chapter are based on studies of the Program-Curriculum Committee and the Section of Life Span Education of The United Methodist Board of Discipleship (and previous Board of Education) in the late sixties and early seventies, and on the sharing of ideas in the Children's Forum in the "Education for Christian Life and Mission Forums" of the National Council of Churches in October, 1975. Ideas have been explored, evaluated, reaffirmed, or revised in working with local church teachers and other church leaders and in personal study and reflection.

2. The Children's Forum was one of several groups in the Education for Christian Life and Mission Forums sponsored jointly by a number of denominations cooperating through the National Council of Churches. The Children's Forum included thirty-five participants from thirteen denominations. These participants were primarily national staff members in denominational agencies concerned with Christian education.

3. The concerns of this paragraph and the following sections on dreams, hopes, purposes, and goals for Christian education are adapted from a paper I wrote, "Christian Education in the 1970's and 1980's." This working paper was developed by a Task Team on Future Program / Resources of the Children's Section of the United Methodist Program-Curriculum Committee.

4. THE LEARNER AND LEARNING

1. The study was made by the Section of Life Span and Family Education of The United Methodist Board of Discipleship (and earlier Board of Education). Some of the developmental resources used in the study were from Erik Erikson, Jean Piaget, Ronald Goldman, Theodore Lidz, and James Fowler.

2. From *Planbook for Leaders of Children, 1978–79* (Nashville: Graded Press, 1978). Copyright © 1978 by Graded Press.

3. This section is based on my article "How Do We Teach Values?" *Planbook for Leaders of Children, 1975–76* (Nashville: Graded Press, 1975).

4. These responses were given in a study group using my unpublished manuscript, "Value Formation as an Aim of the Church's Educational Work."

5. Dorothy Jean Furnish, *Exploring the Bible with Children* (Nashville: Abingdon, 1975), p. 122.

6. *Ibid.*, p. 40.

7. For me as a child and as a young person, mathematical problem-solving with confirmed "right answers" was much easier than learning that required reading-study skills—in fact, I failed geography in the fifth grade. With recognition of my limitations and through further development of study skills, I have found reading extremely beneficial through the years. Other persons' writings have helped me to clarify, reinforce, and revise concepts of the Christian faith and to grow as a learner, a teacher, and a leader in church education.

5. WAYS OF LEARNING, WAYS OF TEACHING

1. The three charts (pp. 35-36), which I developed, are taken from *Planbook for Leaders of Children, 1975–76* (Nashville: Graded Press, 1975), pp. 10-11. Copyright © 1975 by Graded Press.

2. *Teaching Toward Inquiry*, a National Education Association publication, 1971.

3. Adapted from *ibid.*

4. This section is from my article "The Child's Spiritual Growth" in *Planbook for Leaders of Children, 1974–75* (Nashville: Graded Press, 1974), p. 7. Copyright © 1974 by Graded Press.

6. THE TEACHER AND TEACHING

1. "To teach the Bible is to talk about life. To talk about life (within the Christian community) is to teach the Bible." So writes Dorothy Jean Furnish in "Teaching Biblically," a chapter in *Exploring the Bible with Children* (Nashville: Abingdon, 1975). The Furnish book is a good resource for exploring how to bring the Bible and child life together in church school teaching.

2. This section on special needs is adapted from Margie McCarty in *Planbook for Leaders of Children 1977–78* (Nashville: Graded Press, 1977), pp. 6-7. Copyright © 1977 by Graded Press.

7. INVENTING YOUR OWN STYLE OF TEACHING

1. For a listing of activities as distinguished from these general functions, see chapter 9, section on activities, pp. 67-69.

2. See statement p. 55 beginning "A Christian's life is personal."

3. Mary Skinner, *Children's Division Yearbook*, 1950–51. Department of Christian Education of Children, Board of Education, The Methodist Church.

8. USING CURRICULUM MATERIALS AND OTHER RESOURCES

1. This exercise adapted from the leaflet "From Your Point of View," in the *All Aboard Kit* (Nashville: Graded Press, 1975). Copyright © 1975 by Graded Press.

2. For instance, *Foundations of Christian Teaching in United Methodist Churches,* prepared by the Division of Curriculum Resources of the United Methodist Board of Education (Nashville: Graded Press, 1969).

3. Current information is provided in *Planbook for Leaders of Children* (see also *Youth Planbook* and *Adult Planbook*). Each *Planbook,* revised annually, is prepared by the Curriculum Resources Committee and the Board of Discipleship (United Methodist) and printed by Graded Press for free distribution.

4. This section is adapted from my article "Help Teachers Use Curriculum Materials," in *Planbook for Leaders of Children, 1974–75,* pp. 4-5. Copyright © 1974 by Graded Press.

9. PREPARING FOR TEACHING-LEARNING

1. See chapter 5 for a description of the three basic ways of learning, and chapter 10 for interpretation of a variety of approaches in church education.

2. For methods (activities) appropriate for your own age or grade group, see your teacher guidebook and pupil books. For a more inclusive list and interpretation of creative activities, see M. Franklin and Maryann J. Dotts, *Clues to Creativity,* Vols. I-III (New York: Friendship Press, 1974–76).

10. EXPLORING ALTERNATIVE APPROACHES

1. This quotation, and some other key ideas in this section, are from the leaflet "Group Teaching," by LaDonna Bogardus, Workers with Children series. Used by permission of Discipleship Resources, P.O. Box 840, Nashville, Tennessee 37202.

2. These paragraphs from George E. Koehler, *Learning Together—A Guide for Intergenerational Education in the Church* (Nashville: Discipleship Resources, 1977), pp. 14, 10, 14.

3. This series includes four books by Paul B. and Mary Carolyn Maves: *Finding Your Way Through the Bible,* 1970; *Learning More About Your Bible,* 1972; *Exploring How the Bible Came to Be,* 1973; *Discovering How the Bible Message Spread,* 1973 (all published by Graded Press in Nashville).

4. See Bibliography for resources on using learning centers in church education.

11. EVALUATING TEACHING-LEARNING EFFECTIVENESS

1. From Herbert R. Kohl, *The Open Classroom: A Practical Guide to a New Way of Teaching* (New York: The New York Review, 1970), p. 106.

13. THE GROWING TEACHER

1. From Mary Skinner, "Beatitudes for Teachers of Children," *Children's Division Yearbook,* 1950–51. Department of Christian Education of Children, Board of Education, The Methodist Church.

BIBLIOGRAPHY

BOOKS, PACKETS, BOOKLETS

Allstrom, Elizabeth. *You Can Teach Creatively.* Nashville: Abingdon, 1970. $3.95.

Almy, Millie, *et al. Logical Thinking in Second Grade.* New York: Teachers College Press, 1970.

Ames, Louise Bates, and Chase, Joan Ames. *Don't Push Your Preschooler.* New York: Harper, 1974. $6.95.

Anderson, Frances M. *Team Teaching in Christian Education.* Chicago: The Evangelical Covenant Church in America, 1967.

Anderson, Harold H. *Creativity and its Cultivation.* New York: Harper, 1959.

Arnold, Joan, *et al. Journeys Into Faith.* Nashville: Graded Press Study book, $1.50; cassette tape $4.95.

Bower, William Clayton. *Religious Education in the Modern Church.* St. Louis: Bethany Press, 1929. (Out of print.)

Brown, Marion E. *The Learning Center Model as an Option for the Church's Educational Work* (8672C). Nashville: Discipleship Resources, 1974.

Calhoun, Mary. *Vacation Time—Leisure Time—Any Time You Choose.* Nashville: Abingdon, 1974.

Campbell, James M. *Our Faith and Our Teaching.* St. Louis: Christian Board of Publication, 1975.

Despert, J. Louise. *The Inner Voices of Children.* New York: Simon & Schuster, 1975. Cloth $10.95; paper, $3.95.

Dotts, M. Franklin and Dotts, Maryann J. *Clues to Creativity: Providing Learning Experiences for Children.* New York: Friendship Press, 1974-76. $3.95 each; 3 for $4.50.

Drescher, John M. *Seven Things Children Need.* Scottsdale, Pa.: Herald Press, 1976. Paper, $1.95.

Duckert, Mary. *Help! I'm a Sunday School Teacher.* Philadelphia: Westminster, 1969. $1.85

———. *Open Education Goes to Church.* Philadelphia: Westminster, 1970.

E.G's. 8 leaflets summarizing experiments in church education. 1974. Order from Christian Board of Publication, Box 1986, Indianapolis, IN 46206.

Farley, Thomas K. *The Church's Emerging Life as a Source in Shaping Its Educational Work* (8655C). Nashville: Discipleship Resources, 1974.

Flapan, Dorothy. *Children's Understanding of Social Interaction.* New York: Teachers College Press, 1968.

Furnish, Dorothy Jean. *Exploring the Bible with Children.* Nashville: Abingdon, 1975. $3.95.

Gleason, John J., Jr. *Growing Up to God.* Nashville: Abingdon, 1975.

Goddard, Carrie Lou. *The Child and His Nurture.* Nashville: Abingdon, 1962.

Goldman, Ronald. *Readiness for Religion.* New York: Seabury, 1970.

———. *Religious Thinking from Childhood to Adolescence.* New York: Seabury, 1968.

Hall, Arlene S. *Toward Effective Teaching: Elementary Children.* St. Louis: Christian Board of Publication, 1969. Paper, $2.25.

Holland, Bernice C. *How to Individualize Kindergarten Teaching.* Englewood Cliffs, N.J.: Prentice-Hall, 1974.

Holt, John. *How Children Learn.* Belmont, CA.: Pitman, 1967, 1969.

Individualizing Instruction. Association for Supervision and Curriculum Development (ASCD), 1964.

Innovations in Education, New Directions for the American School. Committee for Economic Development, 1968.

Innovations in Education series. Twelve leaflets summarizing some major trends in church education. 10¢ each; 12 for $1.00. Discipleship Resources, Box 840, Nashville, TN 37202. Also request information on titles of *Innovation Packets.* Each packet contains 8 to 10 reports of actual work in a specific educational area.

Isham, Linda. *On Behalf of Children.* Valley Forge: Judson Press, 1975. Paper, $1.50.

Johnson, David W., and Johnson, Frank P. *Joining Together: Group Theory and Group Skills.* Englewood Cliffs, N.J.: Prentice-Hall, 1975.

Jones, Mary Alice. *The Christian Faith Speaks to Children.* Nashville: Abingdon, 1965. Paper, $1.75.

Kemp, Charles F. *Thinking and Acting Biblically.* Nashville: Abingdon, 1976. Paper, $3.50.

Koehler, George E. *Learning Together: A Guide for Intergenerational Education in the Church.* Nashville: Discipleship Resources, 1977.

Kohl, Herbert R. *The Open Classroom.* New York: Vintage books. Paper, $1.65.

The Learning Center Approach in Church Education. Philadelphia: United Church Board of Homeland Ministries, 1971.

Learning in the Small Church. Atlanta: General Assembly Mission

Board. Six booklets including: Meek, Pauline Palmer, *Ministries with Children in Small Churches,* Philadelphia: Geneva Press, 1975; Edgerton, Joan, *Learning Centers,* Atlanta: John Knox Press, 1976; *Learning in Families,* John Knox Press, 1976.

Lee, James Michael. *The Religious Education We Need: Toward the Renewal of Christian Education.* Religious Education, 1977.

Lidz, Theodore. *The Person: His Development Throughout the Life Cycle.* New York: Basic Books, 1968.

Logan, James C. *Theology as a Source in Shaping the Church's Educational Work* (8652C). Nashville: Discipleship Resources, 1974.

Mather, June. *Learning Can Be Child's Play.* Nashville: Abingdon, 1976.

New Forms Exchange. Reports on innovations in educational programs in the local church. For information write to New Forms Exchange, Division of Christian Education, Room 720, United Church Board of Homeland Ministries, 1505 Race St. Philadelphia, PA 19102.

New Ways for New Days, Intergenerational Experiences in Church Education. Philadelphia: Geneva Press, 1976.

Nicholson, Dorothy. *Toward Effective Teaching: Young Children.* Anderson, Ind.: Warner Press, 1970. Paper, $2.25.

Perceiving, Behaving, Becoming. ASCD Yearbook. 1962.

Pitcher, Evelyn G., *et al. Helping Young Children Learn.* 2nd ed. Chicago: Merrill, 1974. For nursery and kindergarten teachers. $6.95.

Planbook for Leaders of Children. Revised annually. Nashville: Graded Press. Available free from Cokesbury. United Methodist. (Also see planbooks or guidebooks of other denominations.)

Prince, George M. *The Practice of Creativity.* New York: Macmillan, 1972.

Rich, John Martin. *Innovations in Education: Reformers and Their Critics.* Boston: Allyn and Bacon, 1975.

Rood, Wayne. *The Art of Teaching Christianity.* Nashville: Abingdon, 1968.

Rowan, Ruth Dinkins. *Helping Children with Learning Disabilities.* Nashville: Abingdon, 1977.

Ryan, Roy H. *Possessing Our Heritage, An Aim of the Church's Educational Work.* Nashville: Discipleship Resources, 1976.

Schisler, John Quincy. *Christian Teaching in the Church.* Nashville: Abingdon, 1954. (Out of print.)

Schmuck, Richard A., and Schmuck, Patricia A. *Group Processes in the Classroom.* Dubuque: Wiliam C. Brown, 1975.

Sellers, James. *Warming Fires.* New York: Seabury, 1975.

Shumsky, Abraham. *In Search of Teaching Style.* Englewood Cliffs, N.J.: Prentice-Hall, 1968.

Tanner, Grace. *They Are Truly Children of God.* Nashville: Discipleship Resources, 1975. $1.00 each; 10 or more, 85¢ each.

Taylor, Marvin. *Foundations for Christian Education in an Era of Change.* Nashville: Abingdon, 1976.

Teaching Toward Inquiry. Washington: National Education Association, 1971.

Tobey, Katherine. *Learning and Teaching Through the Senses.* Philadelphia: Westminster Press, 1970. $3.25.

Torrance, E. Paul, and Myers, R. E. *Creative Learning and Teaching.* New York: Harper, 1970.

Using Learning Centers in Church Education. Richmond: John Knox Press.

Vieth, Paul H. *Improving Your Sunday School.* Philadelphia: Westminster, 1930. (Out of print.)

Wangner, Florence E. *Teaching Bible Concepts.* Valley Forge: Judson Press, 1972.

Weaver, Horace. *Getting Straight About the Bible.* Nashville: Abingdon, 1975.

Westerhoff, John H., III, and Simon, Sidney B. *How Can We Teach Values?* Three article reprints. Philadelphia: United Church Press, 1969. Available from Christian Board of Publication, St. Louis.

———. *Values for Tomorrow's Children.* Philadelphia: United Church Press. 1970. $4.95.

———. *Will Our Children Have Faith?* New York: Seabury, 1976. $6.95.

White, Emma Jane. *Let's Do More with Children.* Nashville United Methodist Board of Education, 1969 (0198-BC). 95¢.

———. *Let's Do More with Persons with Disabilities.* Nashville: United Methodist Board of Education (0131-BC), 1973. $1.00.

Wingeier, Douglas E. *General Education as a Source in Shaping the Church's Educational Work* (8654C). Nashville: Discipleship Resources, 1974.

Workers with Children, series of leaflets. Write to Discipleship Resources and request *Workers with Children: A Bibliography.* Free.

FILMS, FILMSTRIPS, CASSETTES, KITS, MULTIMEDIA NOTEBOOKS

Christian Living with Young Children. Multimedia kit. Nashville: Graded Press, 1975. $9.50.

Communicating the Faith with Children. 4 cassettes, workbook, self-instruction guide. Nashville: The United Methodist Board of Discipleship, 1972. $24.95.

Design for Communication: Learning Center. Nashville: United Methodist Communications. 35mm filmstrip with 33⅓ rpm record.

The Group Way of Teaching. Nashville: The Methodist Board of Education. 35mm filmstrip with 33⅓ rpm record, script, guide. $10.00.

I Can notebooks for teachers and other leaders. Nashville: Discipleship Resources, 1977–78. $8.50 each. Include articles, games, worksheets, leaflets, records, posters, bibliography. McCarty, Margie, and Andre, Evelyn. *I Can Teach Young Children;* McCarty, Margie, *I Can Plan for Ministries with Children;* Maberry, Grace, *I Can Teach Older Elementary Boys and Girls;* Porter, Margaret, *I Can Teach Younger Elementary Children.*

Interaction in the Classroom. Philadelphia: Westminster. Illustrated booklet with 10 separate sheets of illustrations. #70003-9. $2.50

The Joy of Learning, Using Learning Centers. Richmond: John Knox Press. 35mm filmstrip with 33⅓ rpm record, script, and booklet. $6.50.

Ministry with Retarded Persons. Kit including filmstrip, 33⅓ rpm record, resource book, bibliography, and checklist. Nashville: United Methodist Board of Discipleship, 1969. 0502-AV.

Nursery Leadership. 35 mm filmstrip, 2 scripts, guide. Philadelphia: United Church Press. $7.50.

Teaching and Learning series. 16mm films. Philadelphia: Geneva Press. Grades 1-2, Grades 3-4, Grades 5-6. Available from ACI Films, Inc., 35 W. 45th St., New York, NY 10036.

Teaching in the Kindergarten. 35mm filmstrip, script, guide. Philadelphia: United Church Press. $7.50.

Teaching with Learning Centers. 35mm filmstrip with cassette. Griggs Educational Service, Box 362, Livermore, CA 94550.

Teaching Yourself to Teach. Howard Walker. Multimedia kit. Nashville: Abingdon, 1974. $8.95.

Team Teaching. 35mm filmstrip with 33⅓ rpm record and script. Nashville: The United Methodist Board of Education. $9.95.

Ways the Bible Comes Alive in Communicating the Faith. 4 cassettes, workbook, self-instruction guide. Nashville: The United Methodist Board of Discipleship. $29.95.

What Do You Think? 16mm film. Children's concepts. ACI Films, Inc., 35 W. 45th St., New York, NY 10036. Rental, $30.00.

What Will You Do for Libby? 35mm filmstrip, color, 33⅓ rpm record, two scripts, guide. Nashville: Graded Press, 1976.

For information on curriculum materials for the church school, refer to annotated lists in denominational literature and catalogs. These lists include resources for use with persons of various ages and with special learning needs.